Through the VALLEY

No one is absolved from the Burdens
and Misfortunes of Life.

JERMAINE RUDD

k J. Kenkade
PUBLISHING

J. Kenkade Publishing
5920 Highway 5 N. Ste. 7
Bryant, AR 72022
www.jkenkadepublishing.com

J. Kenkade Publishing is a registered trademark.

Printed in the United States of America

ISBN 978-1-955186-56-8

This book recounts actual events in the life of Jermaine Rudd according to the author's recollection and perspective. Some of the identifying details may have been changed to respect the privacy of those involved.

CONTENTS

Acknowledgments

The old saying goes, "When life hands you lemons, make lemonade." It took me thirty-six years of life filled with ups and downs to realize that even the lemonade can also be bitter or sweet.

To everyone who takes the time to read this book, I want you to remember that valleys are not meant to be stayed in but be gone through. Since I know that everyone's valley is not the same, I would like to take this time to acknowledge my family that means more to me than anything in this world.

In many ways, I am the man I am today because of them. It is through my family that I learned how to pray, love, show compassion, and know that God is in control of all things. Therefore, it is my privilege and honor to start this narrative by recognizing them. You all have shown me how it feels to walk through the valley and make it out on the other side.

WRONG TURN

"Everything in your life is a reflection of a choice you have made.
If you want a different result, make a different choice."

N ever giving up, always looking a person in the eye, and never showing weakness are the keys to surviving this life as I was told. Yet, no one told me that life would be so hard and that every decision I would make would have consequences. I was 10 years old when I figured out that growing up was a choice, but getting older was inevitable. It was 1997, and I was just coming into my own. I was the youngest of four siblings. My oldest brother, Gary, moved out of the house when I was 7, leaving my second oldest brother, Val, my sister, Sharri, and myself to fend for ourselves.

We all were raised in a single-parent household, which now has become normalized in a black community. On top of that, it did not make it any better that we grew up in poverty. My mother, Ellane, (God rest her soul), did the best she could trying to raise four eager children on her own. It was not easy for her to carry a disability and have to care for her four children without the ability to see physically. Yes, my mother was legally blind, so I knew I had to grow up quickly for my family. I was a child still trying to figure out where to turn.

Our father was in and out of our home, leaving me to turn to the streets for love, support, and just the feeling of belonging to something or someone. I turned to three guys that I clinched with tightly, Donald, Kevin, and Brent. Just as it was in my own family, I was also the youngest in this group. They welcomed me in quickly, treating me as their little brother. Our bond became so strong that we did everything together, and if one person had something, we all had it.

We were so inseparable that not even blood could have made us closer. I put all my trust in these guys, believing that whatever we did, they would make sure that I was good. Honestly, this also included if we were doing something wrong. Kevin, who was the oldest of the group, made all the decisions. Normally, what he said was never challenged by the rest of us.

'Yes', I thought to myself. 'I finally belong to something'. I had three guys that actually cared about me and treated me like a real little brother. Basically, everything that I was searching and longing for, I was finding in my crew.

As time started to tick and we were getting older, things became expensive for us. Kevin decided that it was time to start making our own way. Our appetites had gotten so big that the little we received from our own parents was no longer fulfilling anymore. One night, during our normal neighborhood stroll, Kevin asked us a question.

"Are you guys tired of being broke?" he asked.

'Yes', I thought to myself but never spoke a word.

"Are you guys tired of asking your parents for money every time you want something, only to hear, "No" or "I do not have it"?" he continued. He had hit the nail on the head with that question, and before I knew it, he then directed his next question toward me.

"Lil'Jay," he called me, which was short for John.

"Yes?" I replied, wondering what his next question would be.

"Your mom is blind, right?"

"Yes," I responded.

"Would you not like to make it easier on her?" he asked.

"Yes, I would," I replied.

"Do you not want to start buying your own clothes and shoes?" he asked.

'I like how this is sounding and going,' I thought to myself.

"Yes, man," I replied. Getting more and more excited, I then asked, "How are we going to do that?" I was not ready for the next response that was getting ready to come out of his mouth.

"By taking what we want," he said. "We will start wearing backpacks," he continued.

"Backpacks?" I replied.

"Yes, empty backpacks," he said.

"Why empty backpacks?" I asked.

"Tomorrow night, everyone bring an empty backpack," Kevin said.

Like I said, we never challenged Kevin, so we all said "OK" and proceeded home.

The next day had arrived, and Donald, Brent, and I were awaiting the arrival of Kevin. We stood there silently with our empty backpacks in hand.

'What could we possibly be doing with these empty backpacks?' I thought to myself. It was way after school hours, and quite frankly, I thought we all looked ridiculous carrying around backpacks at that time of the day. Finally, Kevin arrived with a sneaky and devious smile on his face.

"Come on, guys," Kevin said while moving quickly as if he was in a rush to get somewhere. We all began to walk; however, this time, we were walking faster than usual, with a lot less talking than most times. I decided to break the silence, which was becoming so overwhelming because of the anxiety of thinking about what would be next.

"Kev," I said, which was what we called him for short.

"What's up, Lil'Jay?" he responded.

"What are we going to do with these empty backpacks?" I asked. "We look stupid, I think," I continued.

"Yeah, man, Lil'Jay is right. We look stupid carrying around these empty backpacks," Don said.

"They will not be empty much longer; just wait," Kev responded.

We continued to walk, and it was getting close to nightfall. Every corner we turned on, the street lights began to flicker on. Before I knew it, we were ways away from our normal route.

"Y'all ready?" Kevin asked.

"Ready for what?" we all asked. Kevin started assigning us areas to watch and told Donald to go with him.

"Brent, you and Lil'Jay go by that tree and duck down to look out," Kevin said. "Whistle if you see any lights coming over the hill," he continued. Brent and I did exactly what we were told and ducked down tightly by the tree, not to be seen by the naked eye. We began to watch closely to see what would take place next. I watched Kevin and Donald creep across the street, dipping and dodging in and out behind cars.

'What in the hell are they doing?' I thought to myself. I could not believe my eyes. 'No!' my conscience screamed on the inside! 'Are they really doing this?' I thought to myself.

I even hit Brent on the arm and asked, "Do you see this?"

"Keep looking over the hill," Brent said. I turned to watch Kevin and Donald, and I could not believe it. Up and down, in and out, like two thieves in the night.

'Am I really going to be a part of this?' I thought to myself.

Finally, with a loud whistle, Kevin yelled, "Come on!"

Brent and I jumped up from behind the tree and ran as fast as we could to catch up to Kevin and Donald. We ran non-stop, all the way back to our normal meeting spot, allowing our momentum to carry us all the way. I took a moment to catch my breath from the long run. My heart was racing, and I was panicking with so many thoughts running through my mind.

"Kevin, what are you thinking?" I asked. "What if someone saw us? What if we get caught?" I continued.

"We will not get caught," he replied. "It is dark, and no one saw our faces. Just shut up!" he continued.

I did not know what to say after that. I knew if I spoke against Kevin, I would not be able to hang with them anymore.

'Do I turn to leave and not take part in this foolishness, or do I stay to see what all we took? I cannot risk being alone and without any friends. What would they say about me?' I thought to myself. 'They will probably call me a baby and say I am weak. Can I deal with that?' I pondered. I could not risk losing the family that I longed for for so long.

I stared around at everyone's faces and said what anyone in my position would say: "What did we get?"

Kevin began to pull out all kinds of things, and before I knew it, we were standing with tons of stolen goods.

"What are we supposed to do with all of this?" I asked.

"We will split the cash we have now, and I will find someone to pawn the rest for us and split the remaining cash," Kevin said.

"Where are we going to find someone to pawn all of this without looking suspicious?" I asked.

"I will handle that, just come back tomorrow with your backpacks again," Kevin said.

I went home that night with a puzzled look on my face, thinking about what I just did.

As I walked in the door, my mom asked, as she normally does, "How was your day, son?" I could not tell her what I had just done, but I had never kept a secret from her. I had always been able to share my day with her, but this time, it was different. I was scared, but most of all, I was ashamed. A feeling of discomfort and deceit just rushed through my body.

I looked her in the eyes and answered, "It was good, Mom." I turned away to hide as if I was naked or as if she could actually see right through me. I lay down puzzled that night, asking myself if I could continue to do this, and I slowly drifted to sleep. The next day, after school, we met up at our normal meeting location again. As we patiently waited for Kevin to show up, I began to speak my mind.

"I cannot be a part of this, Don," I said. "It is not right, and we could get caught and go to jail," I continued. "Do you want to go to jail, Don? Do you want your mom to find out what you are doing? What about you, Brent? Are you willing to get put behind bars over a few dollars?" Just as I was talking to Don and Brent, Kevin quickly approached us.

"What are you talking about now, Lil'Jay?" he asked. I decided to speak my mind and let Kevin know how I felt about what we were doing.

"Kevin, this is wrong, and I do not want to be a part of this anymore," I said.

In the middle of my venting, Kevin pulled out a handful of cash and said, "We will split your $100 among the three of us."

I stared down at the $100 and asked, "Is all of this mine?" At the time, $100 was a lot of money for a 13-year-old.

"Yes, all of this is yours if you are with us," he replied.

I stared at the money that Kevin was holding again and did what any 13-year-old kid would do. I took the money and asked, "What's next?"

This went on for a while, and we began to get large. Money was beginning to become a must-have for us. The more money we got, the more popular we grew. In my heart, I knew it was wrong, but the ability to have my own money and not depend on my mom overruled my heart. We had gotten so good at it that we moved to different neighborhoods. What was once $100 turned into $300 a week, and for a 13-year-old who did not have much growing up, that was the life. It became more and more easy to look at my mom in the face and lie every day. All this was for the love of money.

chapter

2

FIRST TIME FOR EVERYTHING

*"The first step to getting what you want is to have
courage to get rid of the things you don't."*

It was 1998, and everything seemed to be falling right into place for me. I had money, clothes, shoes, and fame, but most of all, I had my friends who were like brothers. As a 14-year-old kid, what more could I ask for? Our popularity was so big that our names became known all around the schools. At school, we were known as The Crew.

I would always think to myself, 'What could be better than this?'

One night, the guys and I decided to take the night off from our normal activities that seemed to bring us so much wealth. I walked up to Kevin's house since he lived a few houses down from me.

"What's up, Kevin?" I asked as we both stood in the doorway

to greet each other. "What are you doing tonight since we are off?" I asked.

"I think I am going to have Michelle come over," he said.

Michelle was Kevin's girlfriend; well, at least some days, she was. They had a weird relationship that I did not quite understand at times.

Sometimes, she was all Kevin would talk about, but then there were other days he would say, "Michelle who?" as if she was a total stranger. I guess you could say that they had a love/hate relationship.

Michelle came over while I was sitting in the living room watching television. "Hey, Lil'Jay," she said.

"What's up, Michelle?" I replied.

"Sooo, Lil'Jay," she began to speak.

"Yes?" I replied.

"When are you going to give my girl, Porsha, a chance? You know that she is crazy about you."

Porsha was cool, but I never thought about being in a relationship with her.

"I do not know," I replied. "She is too clingy for me," I said.

As she began to talk more to me about Porsha, Kevin interrupted and said, "Are you here to play matchmaker or to see me?" As I laughed, Kevin and Michelle walked back to his room to have their privacy. That was fine because I just continued to watch the game while they went to the back for privacy.

A few minutes into halftime, I decided to get up and go into the kitchen for some snacks. I opened up the refrigerator to grab a soda when I began to hear a sound that stopped me dead in my tracks.

"Are they… Could they…? No, they cannot be," I said to myself, easing closer and closer to Kevin's door. The sound started to get louder, and I could hear the knocking of the bed frame as if it were trying to come through the walls. Yes, it was true, Kevin and Michelle were doing the big IT, the twirlie girlie, the naked tango; they were having sex.

After listening by the door for a few minutes, I ran and jumped back on the couch as if I had been there the whole time.

They finally came out of the room and Michelle said, "I guess I will let you get back to your company."

"Okay, see you at school tomorrow," Kevin said, giving her a big, long, passionate kiss as if he was ready to go back into the room for another round.

"See you later, Lil'Jay," she said. Kevin then came back and sat by me to watch the game. Complete silence took over the atmosphere as if the game had both of our attention.

Enough was enough; I had to break the ice.

"Michelle did not stay long," I said.

"No, she had to go pick up her little sister," he replied.

"Sooo, what were you guys doing in there?" I asked jokingly.

"What do you think we were doing in there?" he asked with a smile on his face.

My next question was only to justify and confirm that the sounds I had heard from behind his door were certain.

"Was it good?" I asked.

He laughed and said, "I would not be with her if it wasn't."

We both laughed at each other, and before I knew it, he asked me a question that I was not ready for.

"Are you still a virgin, Lil'Jay?"

My laugh was completely cut off, and I took a deep, long pause, thinking to myself, 'Do I tell him the truth? I cannot tell him that I am still a virgin. I never have gone past first base with a girl. He will laugh at me for sure. I mean, what is the big deal about it? It is only sex, right? I mean, we really should not be having sex, anyway.'

After a million thoughts ran through my mind, I finally replied, "Yes, I am still a virgin."

"That is cool," he said. "I already knew you were, just wanted to see if you would be honest with me."

It was a Friday night, and we had a big basketball game at home. Kevin, who played on the varsity team, had to be at the gym early. Donald, Brent, and I would normally come later when it was closer to time for the boy's game to start. As we walked into the gym, we ran into Michelle, Porsha, and their friend, Lisa.

"Hey, guys," they all uttered at the same time.

"What's up, ladies?" Donald and I replied.

As I slowly walked toward the concession stand, I heard a loud, annoying voice say, "See you later, Lil'Jay."

Porsha had her way of making her presence felt whenever she was around us.

When the game started, Donald, Brent, and I sat in our normal spot at the very top of the bleachers. We sat there so that we could see who walked in the gym and also keep our eyes on the game at the same time. During halftime, Michelle, Porsha, and Lisa came to the top and sat by us.

"So, Lil'Jay," Michelle said.

"What's up, Michelle?" I replied.

"What are you guys doing after the game tonight?" she asked.

Normally, after a home game, we would all go to McDonalds, which was our hangout location before moving on to the next place. "I guess we will go to McDonalds as always, but after that, I am not sure," I replied. "What about you guys?" I extended the question back to her.

Michelle had a smile that would make you question her very thoughts. It was as if you knew she was up to something because her face would tell it all. "Well, we were thinking about staying around here after the game," she said.

'Why would they stay at the school when the game was over?' I thought to myself.

"Kevin said you guys were staying, too," she said as her smile grew even more devious. "I am sure Kevin will let you guys know the plan, so make sure you are ready, Lil'Jay," she continued. She, Porsha, and Lisa then got up to walk back to their original seats to watch the rest of the game.

"What was that all about?" I asked Donald and Brent.

"I guess we will just have to wait for Kevin," Donald replied. By this time, the fourth quarter had started for the boy's game. I tried to focus on the game, but all I could think about was what Michelle had said to me at halftime. What could we possibly do here after hours? Even more, what did she mean by telling me to make sure I was ready? What would I need to be ready for? As the clock slowly ticked down and the game was getting closer and closer to the end, Donald, Brent, and I made our way down by the locker to meet Kevin. As soon as the buzzer went off, Kevin ran down to the locker room and told us to stay there until he got dressed. While we were waiting on Kevin to get dressed, we watched everyone start to leave the gym.

"Come on," Kevin said. We then walked to the back of the gym, and Kevin put a small rock in the door, preventing it from latching shut.

"Why are you leaving the door cracked?" I asked.

"So we can get back in, Lil'Jay," he replied. "Trust me, it will be worth it tonight," he continued with a smirk on his face. We began

13

to walk toward the convenience store that we often went to during school lunch.

"Are we not going to McDonalds?" I asked.

"No, you are getting ready to do something even better," Kevin replied.

Then suddenly, Kevin's phone rang. "Hello, yes, you guys ready?" he asked the person on the other end of the phone. Who was he talking to?

'What would be better than going to McDonalds?' I thought to myself. Kevin hung up his phone and looked back at us.

"You guys ready to head back?" he asked.

"Sure," Donald replied.

Slowly, we began to walk back toward the gym when I saw three shadows approaching over the hill. The closer we got, the more I began to hear the laughter of female voices echoing in the shadows.

"Hey, guys," Michelle said as she and Kevin greeted each other with a passionate kiss like he wanted to rip her clothes off right there. We all started walking back toward the gym, and I noticed Porsha and Michelle giggling as if they were planning to do something sneaky.

"Lil' Jay," Kevin said.

"What's up?" I replied.

"Tonight you become a man, lil' bro," he said as he slid a small plastic wrapper into my hand.

"What is this Kevin, and what do you mean tonight I "become a man?" I asked.

"Trust me, you will need this tonight," he said.

I opened my hand to see what Kevin had secretly slid into the palm of my hand: *Trojan. America's #1 trusted condom.* My heart began to pound, and my hands started to sweat.

"Kevin, this is a condom."

"Duh," he replied.

"But Kev—" I said.

"No buts, Lil'Jay, unless it is Porsha's butt," he laughed while hitting me continuously.

'What do I do now?' I thought to myself. 'Do I turn away and just go home? Do I just say no and give this round object back to him? I know I will look soft if I do. They would probably call me a chicken.'

So, I did what I felt a person in my position would do. I slid the condom into my pocket and said, "Let's go."

As we made our way back to the gym, Kevin slowly slid the rock out of the door and told us to wait. He walked inside and slowly pulled the door up behind him. Two minutes later, he came back and said, "Okay, guys, the coast is clear." We all crept into the gym one by one, trying our best to not make a sound. I gently closed the door behind me. "Come with me," Kevin said.

As I watched Porsha and Michelle walk behind us, my hands began to shake thinking about what was about to happen next. I slowly walked into the locker room with Porsha closing in tightly behind me. When I turned around, she slapped a big, long, and wet kiss on me as if she had been craving this moment for a long time. She began to undress as my hands slowly caressed her coke-bottle frame. Still nervous about what was happening, I started to get more and more comfortable enduring what was getting ready to take place. The temperature started to rise, and my body quickly reacted to every touch. Porsha pulled me on top of her while kissing me passionately.

"Wait, I have to do something," I said. I dug in my pocket to pull out the pack that I had received from Kevin.

Porsha then grabbed it and said, "Let me put it on." Being that I had never put one on before, I was happy to oblige. She gently slid it onto me and pulled me closer to her.

'This is it,' I thought to myself. 'I cannot believe I am doing this.' I knew it was wrong, but it felt so right. 'I guess Kevin was right when he said tonight I become a man.'

chapter

3

FIGHT TO THE END

"The hardest battle you will ever have to fight is between who you are now and who you want to become."

Summer was quickly approaching, and our time together as a crew was slowly coming to an end. Kevin and Donald were a few weeks away from graduating high school. Brent started to find himself in trouble quite often, which caused him to be absent for long periods of time. As for me, I would like to say that I was becoming my own man. Things did not last long between Porsha and me, as I feared from the beginning. I knew that she would easily get attached, and I was not quite ready for that. She wanted to be together before school, during school, and after school. Honestly, I admit that I did have feelings and cared for Porsha, but who really has time for that? We were still able to remain friends and even see each other every once in a while.

I also started a new job working at Frank's Therapy and Gym. I would work there four days a week: Tuesday, Wednesday, Thursdays after school, and Saturday mornings. I enjoyed the fact that I was making an honest living that did not require me to be out at all times of the night. I did not have to look over my back or even worry about getting stopped and asked what was in my backpack.

Since I also played ball, I was able to work out before leaving to go home. Some days, I would even allow Kevin and Donald to come up to the gym and work out for free since it was close to our house.

Things were looking up for me and the crew despite Brent's line of trouble. Our success had made us quite envies in the eyesight of other crews. All the guys wanted to be like us, and all the girls wanted to be with us. I hate to brag, but we were the most popular crew in high school. By this time, we all had girlfriends, and our time together as a crew seemed to lessen more and more. We still found opportunities to meet up, but most of the time, it was on the weekends. Steadily, we were not a crew that caused trouble, but trouble seemed to find us at times.

Summer was now here, and the best thing about the summer was the big pool parties. That summer, everyone knew that Lakita's pool party would be the biggest party of the summer. We had been planning for this party before school ended. Lakita was a good friend of ours and was also one of the most popular girls in school. We knew that Kita's party would definitely be a hit and one for the ages. Brent, Donald, Kevin, and I decided to meet up a week before the party to buy new swim gear.

"So, Lil'Jay, what color trunks are you getting for the party?" Kevin asked.

"I think I am going with the black and gold ones," I replied.

"Let's all go with the black and gold ones," Donald suggested. We all grabbed our trunks and proceeded to the register to pay for them.

As we made our way to the register, in walked Michelle and Porsha.

"Hey, guys," they both greeted us.

"What's up, ladies?" we all replied.

"Hey, Lil'Jay," Porsha said, seemingly being extra. She always knew how to make her presence felt.

"What's up, Porsha?" I replied.

"Are you guys going to Kita's party?" Michelle asked.

Before we all could answer, Kevin jumped in and said, "You know we are not missing this party. "Plus, I cannot have these guys looking at that sexy body without me being there," he continued." We all laughed at Kevin as he seduced and stared at Michelle.

"So, Lil'Jay?"

"Yes, Porsha?" I replied.

"Is your girlfriend coming?" she asked.

"No, she will be out of town for the summer," I replied.

"Too bad, looks like you are all mine this summer," she said.

Without responding to Porsha's shenanigans, I grabbed my bag and walked out of the store. Michelle and Porsha followed us as we all gathered outside of the store.

"You guys do know the boys from the East side will be there, right?" Porsha said. This was very important information to know. As I mentioned earlier, we were not the most liked crew. For some odd reason, we did not get along well with the guys from the east side. I am not absolutely sure why to this day.

Kevin then looked at Porsha and said, "So what? They are coming to our side of town, and we are not running."

"I am just saying be careful," Porsha replied.

As we all walked away, I asked Kevin, "Do you think there will be trouble at Kita's party?"

"What does it matter, Lil'Jay?" he replied. "This is our side of town, and no one is going to run us out of our home," he continued.

As the days flew by, all I could think about was how big this party was going to be.

Saturday had now arrived, and we were ready to get our party on. This day seemed to feel a little different. You would think that we were preparing for our school prom. The party started at six o'clock, but we all decided to meet up at five. I walked down to Kevin's house since he and I lived close to each other. Donald and Brent's house was on the way to the park, so we met up at Donald's house.

"Everybody good?" Kevin asked.

"Yes," we all responded. As Kevin proceeded to give us a pep talk, I started to think about what Porsha said at the store.

"Alright, fellas, you all know the deal," Kevin said.

"We came together, and we leave together. Never walk anywhere by yourself, not even to the bathroom," he continued. He always finished with this last statement, "If one fights, we all fight." We lived by a certain code growing up. Our loyalty and bond was unmatched and not to be tried. Yes, we had our disagreements, but we always returned back to reconcile our differences.

We began to walk toward the park, and many cars heading the same direction passed us. The closer we got to the park, the more we could hear the music playing from the pool area. We finally made our way over the hill, and the parking lot was filled with cars.

"Wow," said Brent. "I knew it was going to be live but not like this," he continued. I was thinking the same as Brent. There were people everywhere, and as soon as we walked onto the pool deck, we were quickly approached.

"What's up, guys?" said Jesse, Collin, and Derrick. These were also guys that I went to school with.

"Nothing much," we all replied.

"Where is Kita?" Donald asked. Before they could even answer, we heard a loud voice coming from the back.

"Hey, guys," Kita said.

I turned around to see that Kita was looking amazing. She was so beautiful to me, and I secretly had the biggest crush on her. She had pretty melanin skin, big brown eyes, long hair, and sexy lips, just to say the least.

"Close your mouth, Lil'Jay," Kevin said as they laughed at me admiring Kita.

I knew I had a girlfriend, but there was something about Kita that always made me weak when I saw her.

"I am so glad you guys made it," she said while looking at me with those beautiful brown eyes. "Hey, Lil'Jay," she addressed her attention toward me.

"What's up, Kita?" I replied.

"Is your girlfriend coming?" she asked.

"No, she is out of town for the summer," I replied.

"Well, too bad for her," she said with a sneaky grin on her face. "Well, I hope you guys enjoy my party," she said as she walked away to greet other people.

As the night went on, the party began to pick up, with more and more people showing up. There were also people who did not attend our school and some who graduated years ago. As the place began to thicken, Kevin thought it would be a great idea to leave early to avoid the crowd when leaving. Making our way towards the exit, I noticed the crowd began to shift toward our direction.

"I guess everyone had the same idea," I said as we continued to walk towards the gate. Without really addressing what I said, Kevin responded by telling us to tie our shoes.

'Why would he say that?' I looked over and saw Brent and Donald lacing their shoes as tight as could be. I bent down to follow suit, and before I knew it, the whole party followed us outside.

We made our way to the bridge that would take us over the hill where we lived. I suddenly heard a loud voice shout, "Look out!", and I turned to see a fist coming directly toward me. I ducked to avoid the contact and to see who would try to hit me. It was the guys from the east side. They outnumbered us at least 15 to 4, and it seemed as if they were steadily coming toward us. Another fist came my way, but this time, I countered it with a punch of my own.

BOOM! I connected, knocking one guy to the ground. I turned around, and I noticed Brent on the ground with six guys on top of him. I ran over to help Brent, and the crowd began to shift. Kevin was fighting two people, and Donald had his hands full as well. This was definitely a battle that did not favor us. I was able to get them off of Brent and stand him back to his feet.

BOOM! There was another blow as I started to swing, connecting with whoever I could. Ten minutes had passed, and I wondered when would this ever end. How long could we stand our ground? We were punching, kicking, scratching, clawing, and biting at that point. Whatever it took to survive.

'How are we going to get out of this one?' Before we knew it, lights were coming over the hill. 'Finally,' I thought to myself, 'Someone is here to stop this.' Hoping to see who was pulling up to us, out jumped more guys from the east side. 'We are going to die tonight,' I thought to myself. So, we all decided to group up by standing back to back.

"If we are going out, we are going out fighting," Kevin said. More lights began to come over the hill, and I thought to myself, 'Not more guys.'

No, this time, it was our own people. It was an older crew that lived in our neighborhood.

"We've got you guys," they said as they all jumped out of multiple cars. They all walked up to join us, and now the battle had just begun.

chapter

4

BETRAYAL

"Sometimes the people closest to you betray you and your home isn't a place you can be happy anymore. It's hard but it's true."

I t was my senior year of high school, and things were falling into place. Kevin and Donald had gone off to college but later decided that college was not for them. Brent never went to college because he found himself in and out of jail for foolish things. Kevin moved back home and decided to work at his family's restaurant. Donald moved in with Brent and his baby mama until he was able to get back on his feet. As for me, it was becoming time for me to make a decision on what college I was going to play ball at.

I was a pretty good baseball player, if I do say so myself. Four-year Letterman, three-year All-State and All-Conference, and All-Star Select were just a few of my accolades. I knew whatever decision I made moving forward would somehow be one of the most important decisions of my life. I decided to take some time to sit down with

Lacy and discuss where our relationship was headed. I really cared about Lacy and believed she cared about me as well. I knew there was a possibility that she would move after graduation. Her mother moved, leaving her to stay with her grandmother until she finished school. I was not sure if she had any plans after high school since she never mentioned what she would like to do.

I always hoped that we would attend the same school and later get married and have a family of our own. Lacy and I had been together for a few years now, and it did not seem as if it would be any different moving forward. I think our relationship was so dynamic because we shared similar interests. She was also athletic and participated in sports and cheerleading. However, I was yet to know if she wanted to pursue that further or if she wanted to go in a different direction. I called her over so that we could talk about our future plans.

"Hey, babe, how are you?" I asked as she walked into my room.

"Hey, Jay, baby," she replied while kissing me passionately.

"Can we talk?" I asked.

"Yes, baby, what do you want to talk about?" she replied.

"As you know, signing day is coming up, and I have to make a decision about where I want to attend school," I said.

"I see," she replied.

"What I am trying to ask, baby, is what your plans are after high school?"

"I am not sure what my plans are," she replied. "I know you will go off to college and forget about me," she continued. "You are this big baseball star, and I am just this average girl with nothing going for herself," she continued.

As I listened more and more to Lacy venting and expressing how she was feeling, I quickly realized that this conversation was not going the way I had planned.

"But baby," I replied.

"No, let me finish," she said.

"You are going to meet some other girl at college, and that will be the end of us," she continued.

"No, baby, that is not true at all," I replied.

"You know what, Jay?" she asked. "Why don't I just leave you alone and save us both the heartache?" she said.

"But babe—" I tried to respond.

Before I knew it, she was walking out the door.

'What just happened?' I asked myself. I stood there puzzled and shocked at what just transpired between Lacy and me. We had had a few minor hiccups, but I had never seen her respond the way that she did that day. Normally, when we had a problem, we would talk about it and later on try to fix or correct it, but this time it felt different. Maybe she was upset about something else and took it out on me. Nevertheless, I knew that at some point, we would talk about it and make amends.

I wanted to call her just to see if she was okay and if there was something I could do. Then again, I wanted to give her time to cool off and hoped that she would later call me to clear the air or share what seemed to bother her most. As I contemplated back and forth on what I should do, I decided to just wait for her to call me when she was ready.

'Surely, we will be able to work through this,' I thought to myself.

After having that crazy conversation with Lacy, I decided to meet up with Kevin and Donald in the hopes of either clearing my mind of the things with Lacy or getting a second opinion on what I may have done wrong. At this point, Brent was back in jail again for allegedly trying to sell stolen car parts. As we got older and our lifestyle changed, I guess with Brent, it was hard to let go of the old lifestyle. It did not help any that Brent never had anything else going for himself. Kevin and Donald played football, and I played baseball, of course. Brent seemed to have more time on his hands to be idle. We all know that the idle mind is the devil's workshop.

I met up with Kevin and Donald at Kevin's house.

"What's up, Kevin, Donald?" I greeted them as I was walking on the steps.

"What's up, Lil'Jay?" they replied. "Where are you coming from?" Donald asked.

"Man, I just had the craziest conversation with Lacy," I replied.

"What do you mean?" Kevin asked.

"Well, I wanted to talk to her about her plans after high school, and she just flipped out on me."

"What did she say?" Donald asked.

"She just started talking about how I was going to go off to college and leave her," I replied. "She even mentioned that I was this big baseball star and that she was this average girl," I continued.

"Well, what do you expect, Lil'Jay?" Kevin asked. "Everyone knows that you are the #3 player in the country, and you have all the major schools recruiting you," he continued. "That is a lot for her to take in, your ceiling being so high. Now, look at Lacy. She quit basketball and got kicked off the track team. Also, let's really be honest, Lil'Jay, I know that is your girl, but she's not the sharpest knife in the drawer when it comes to school." Kevin had his way of being brutally honest. He never bit his tongue on how he felt or how he saw things.

"I know you are right, Kevin," I replied. "I just hope we can talk and work it out soon."

"You guys will be alright," Donald added. "What we need to talk about is this party after the game Friday night," Donald continued.

"Yeah, Lil'Jay, it is your senior night," Kevin said. "It's your last regular season home game, and everyone will be in town to see you," he continued. "Then, you know the after-party is going to be ridiculous."

"I know, Kevin," I said. As I thought more about it, I thought maybe this weekend's party was what Lacy and I needed since we had not been out together in a while. Oftentimes, my weekends were occupied with recruiting trips.

(Ring, Ring) Donald's phone was going off while we were having a brotherhood moment. *(Ring, Ring)* again his phone interrupted us.

"Man, Donald, someone is blowing you up. Must be a new boo," I said jokingly.

"Nobody important," he replied. "So, who's driving to the party?" he asked, quickly changing the subject.

"You guys can just meet at my house after the game," Kevin said. "Lil'Jay, just bring a change of clothes, and you can stay at my house that night," he continued. "Maybe Lacy could come over, and you guys could officially make up if you know what I mean." Kevin was always trying to play Love Jones or Doctor Phil when it came to relationships.

Game day had finally arrived, and I was locked in to finish on top of my game. I had not heard from Lacy in a few days. Even when I called, her phone kept going to voicemail. Other than that, I had a feeling that night was going to be a really good night. We would eventually make up, and everything would go back to normal. Maybe then, she would even surprise me at my game, being that it was my last one at home.

It was the bottom of the 9th, and the bases were loaded. We were down 3-1 as I made my way to the plate.

'I wonder if Lacy is watching,' I thought to myself. 'Focus Jay,' I told myself as my thoughts continued to go back and forth. *(Strike 1)*

I swung and missed. 'Maybe she is watching me from the sky box.' *(Strike 2)* Another swing and miss.

I could not seem to get Lacy out of my head as my coach yelled, "Time!" from the dugout. He walked up to me and said, "What's wrong, son?"

"My mind is just all over the place, Coach," I replied.

"I understand," he said. "Look over there," he pointed to my teammates. "Those guys are depending on you," he continued. "Now, look over there," he pointed toward my family and friends. Those people are here just for you," he added.

"So, what are you saying, Coach?" I asked.

"Focus on those who depend on you and are here for you because, in the end, that is all that matters," he said while walking back to the dugout.

Coach's words resonated deeply with me, and I knew exactly what I needed to do. I walked back up to the plate, focused on the next play, as my mom would always say.

'Here it comes.'

SMACK I fully connected this time and the crowd went wild.

"HOME RUN!" I made my way to home plate, and I was met by my teammates and family. I realized that Coach was right. This was all that mattered.

After the game, we met up at Kevin's house, and I took a shower and changed clothes for the party. I checked my phone to see if I had a missed call or maybe a message from Lacy, only to see that I still had not heard from her.

Well, it was party time, and Kevin, Donald, and I were fashionably late, as usual.

"What's going on, guys?" people greeted us walking in.

"Congratulations, Lil'Jay," I heard a female voice standing behind me. I turned and looked to see who it was, and Porsha was standing there with a huge smile on her face.

"Thanks, Porsha," I replied.

"No problem, you know I would not miss it for the world," she said.

"I know, Porsha, you have always been a true supporter," I replied.

"Good, as long as you know. And by the way, your girl is here," she continued.

"Oh, yeah, where?" I asked.

I then started to hear a loud noise from the center of the room, and I started to make my way over to see what was going on.

Suddenly, I was stopped by Kevin, and he said to me, "Let's go, Lil'Jay."

"Why do we need to go when we just got here?" I asked.

"Let's just go back to Kevin's house," Donald added.

"Man, you guys are tripping. This party is live," I said. "We should go over there where all the excitement is," I added.

As I started my way over again, Kevin stopped me and said, "Wait, Jay."

"What is it now, Kevin?" I asked. It was probably some people having a dance battle. I made my way through the crowd, and I saw two people grinding on the dance floor.

"Man, she is really putting it on him," I said. They might as well have been having sex on the dance floor. After the song was over, they both raised up, and she kissed him passionately as if they were the only ones in the room. I moved to the side to see who could possibly be drawing so much attention.

'No, I cannot believe this!' It was her; it was Lacy!

After being betrayed by Lacy, I really did not know what to think. I was not sure if I would ever trust, let alone love, again. As many times as I could have stepped out on her, I never went there with anyone else. She had called me several times since I saw her at the party, but I knew I was not ready to face her. I did not want to hear the lies or excuses she would come up with.

'What could she possibly have to say? She slipped and landed on his lips after allI did for her? I even wanted to include her in my future plans. If she did not want to be in a relationship, why couldn't she just tell me that? Why did she have to embarrass me like that?' I just could not wrap my mind around why.

Kevin came over to see me because I had not spoken to him or Donald much since the party.

"How are you feeling, Lil'Jay?" Kevin asked.

"Man, Kevin, I do not even know at this point," I said. "I feel confused, hurt, in disbelief, but most of all betrayed," I continued.

"I can imagine, man," Kevin said.

"That is why Donald and I were trying to stop you," he continued. "Plus, you are getting ready to be a pro baseball player soon, Lil'Jay, and you do not need any distractions," Kevin added.

"I guess you are right," I replied.

"Hey, guess what?" Kevin said.

"What?" I replied."

"Brent is coming home today," he said. Brent had been locked up for a while, so it was great to know he was coming home. Things were starting to get better, knowing that our crew was going to be whole again before I left off for college.

"Where is Donald?" I asked.

"He said he had to handle something at the house," Kevin replied. "I am not sure what he had to handle since he is staying with Brent and his lady," he added.

The night had come, and I finally received a phone call from

Brent. I was excited to see his name come across my screen, so I answered with the expectation that he would be excited, too.

"Lil'Jay," he said.

"What's up, Brent?" I replied. "Tell me that you are my brother," he continued.

"What do you mean, Brent?" I asked. "You know that we are brothers for life," I added.

"Tell me that you would never betray me," he said. At this point, I was getting worried. I had never heard Brent talk like this. He was normally laughing and joking around. This was different; I could hear the hurt and sorrow in his voice.

"What is going on, Brent?" I asked again.

"It is Donald," he replied.

"What about Donald?" I asked. "Is he hurt? Is something wrong?"

"Him and my girl have been messing around the whole time I was gone," he said. I was lost for words. I could not believe what I was hearing. That was the ultimate bro code that we did not break. Surely, there had to be some misunderstanding.

"No way, Brent," I said. "You guys are closer than all of us," I continued. "There is no way Donald would do that to you," I continued. "How did you find out?" I asked.

"They both told me," he replied.

"Wait, let's talk to Kevin about this. I am sure he can clear all of this up," I said.

Before I could call Kevin, Brent stopped me and said, "Kevin knew the whole time." I could not believe what was going on and what I was hearing. This was supposed to be a great weekend and homecoming celebration, but instead, it turned out to be the biggest betrayal of them all.

chapter

5

COLLEGE MAN

*"The aim of the college, for the individual student, is
to eliminate the need for the college in his life; the task
is to help him become a self-educating man."*

Move-In Day was here, and I could not be more ready to start this new journey. My mom cried extra hard that time. Maybe it was because I was the last child to leave the nest. My sister and brothers had all gone off to college, but none of them finished. It is funny that I said that because my mom always preached to us about finishing what we started. Things were a little different now after the situation between the crew. We never quite bounced back after the betrayal between Donald and Brent.

Personally, I was still battling with forgiving Donald myself. I trusted him just as well as Brent. I knew that it was more directed toward Brent, but I felt as if he betrayed us all. I talked to him afterward, but it was not the same. I even met up with Kevin to confront him about knowing about the whole thing. He shared with me his reason for not telling me, which was because he knew I would flip out. He claimed that he told Donald he was wrong and that he should leave the house while Brent was gone. I guess the urges and temptations were so strong that he could not fight it. I guess this was a true example of keeping your enemies close and your friends even closer.

As for me and Lacy, I eventually talked to her after seeing her at the party. I was still hurt by what she did, but I knew I had to forgive her at some point. Truth be told, I loved Lacy and would do anything for her. She moved in with her mom after graduation, which was what I expected. She came to see me off and wish me well as I was packing my bags. There was just something about Lacy that I could not let go. I knew that I would meet other people once I got to college, but Lacy would always hold a special place in my heart. "A fool in love" is what they call it now.

As I said my goodbyes to my family, I realized that I would soon be alone again. I was so used to having my crew with me that it felt uncommon to move without them. Nevertheless, I knew that I was here for a purpose and that this would be a new beginning for me. I had promised my mom that I would not only go to college, but I would also be the first one to graduate. I set a goal for myself and wanted to achieve it by any means.

I finally arrived at my school, and I saw the amazing campus and Greek letters everywhere. With a deep sigh, I took in the college air and began to unload my bags and carry them up to my dorm room. While unloading, I saw a sign that read, "Welcome, all freshmen, come chill by the grill at the meet and greet! FREE FOOD."

'First day on the campus, and I already can get free food,' I thought. 'I think I am going to love college after all.'

During the meet and greet, I decided to stand in the back to avoid unwanted attention. Being social was never my strong suit, which was why my circle stayed pretty small. After the situation with my last crew, I did not think I would ever let anyone get that close to me again.

Before I could finish my food, I heard a voice from behind me say, "How's it going, Jay?" I turned around to see who it could be that knew me as Jay. I mean, only my family and friends called me that. To my delight, three familiar faces caught me by surprise.

It was Jessee, Colin, and Derrick, the guys that I also went to school with. Jesse was a big-time basketball player, while Colin and Derrick both played football.

"What's up, guys?" I replied. "I did not know you guys were coming here," I added.

"I received a basketball scholarship," Jessie said.

"Of course, you know Derrick and I came for football," Colin said.

"We figured if Lil' Jay chose this school to carry out his baseball career, then it must be a pretty good place to be," Derrick said. We all laughed as we left the meet and greet to stroll around the campus.

A few months had passed, and things were starting to look pretty good. I finished the first semester by making the Dean's list, and I also won the starting pitcher position for my team. On top of all that, I seemed to have found myself in another solid crew with Jesse, Colin, and Derrick. Who would have ever thought I would have found myself back in a brotherhood situation? After the stain of what Donald left on us, I was skeptical of trusting anyone again. I guess it is true that God knows exactly what you need and when you need it. I could not have imagined things getting any better, or so I thought. Jesse and I decided to walk across campus while Derrick and Colin finished football practice.

"Man, whatever happened to you and Lacy?" Jesse asked. "I thought you guys would never break up," he continued.

"It is a long story," I replied. "I mean, we're still friends, but that is about it," I added.

"Well, we are college men now. I am sure you will find someone else in no time," Jesse said.

"I do not know about that, man, Lacy and I were pretty close," I replied.

We continued to walk across campus when Jesse stopped two girls who seemed to have the same idea as us.

"Hey, ladies, my name is Jesse, and this is my boy, Jay," Jesse said as he introduces us.

"My name is Beth, and this is my girl, Kiera," she replied.

"So, where are you guys from?" Jesse asked.

"We are from Ouachita. What about you guys?" Beth asked.

"We are from Hempstead," I replied.

"I know some people from Hempstead," Kiera said. "Do you know a guy named Jaleel?" she asked.

"Yes, that is my cousin," I said.

"Really?" she said. With excitement in her voice, she said, "He is married to my cousin."

Before I knew it, Kiera and I were connecting on a major level. The connection I thought Lacy and I had was nothing compared to Kiera and me. We laughed and talked for hours about any and everything. Kiera was not only becoming the love I longed for, but she was also becoming my best friend. We would meet each other after class, and I would walk her back to her dorm room. When neither one of us had class, we would sit outside the dorms by the swings and talk about life and what we wanted to do. As Kiera and I grew closer, it seemed that everything was falling into place. I could not imagine life any better than this.

Suddenly, I was approached by these guys dressed in gold and black colors, with letters and symbols on their chests.

"You are John, the baseball pitcher, right?" one of them asked.

"Yes," I replied. "Man, we've been watching you for a while. You are some kind of pitcher," he continued.

"I appreciate you guys," I responded.

"So, what are you throwing nowadays, 101mph?" he asked.

"103, actually," I replied.

"Man, that is fast. Well, I am K.C., President of Alpha Sigma Delta, and these guys are my frat brothers," he said. "We are having an interest meeting tonight, and we would like for you to come check it out," he continued. I never thought about joining a fraternity. Playing ball was all I knew, but how cool would it be to join a fraternity in the process?

"I will be there," I replied.

"Great. We will get started at 9:06pm, and do not be late," he said.

As the day went by, all I could think about was the interest meeting that night. I decided to link up with Kiera to share the good news with her. She seemed just as excited as I was and also shared an interest in possibly joining a sorority. By this time, I knew Kiera and I had a special bond that would be hard to break. We shared similar interests in everything. The night had come, and I decided to head over to the meeting around 8:50 p.m. It was about a 5-minute walk across campus, but I wanted to make sure I was not late.

I soon approached the room and was greeted by a few guys that I saw around the campus. They all seemed so nervous, walking around, pacing the floor back and forth.

"You are John, the baseball player, right?" one of them asked.

"Yes," I replied.

"They are definitely going to select you," he said. I really did not understand the point of being so nervous. It was not a life or death situation, nor was it going to be the end of the world.

I tried to relax the room by saying, "Hey, guys, if we make it, we make it, and if we do not make it, then that is okay, too."

"Alright, everybody, sit down," K.C said as he walked into the room. "If you are interested in any other fraternity or think you are interested, now is the time to leave," he continued. We all just stared around, looking to see if anyone would leave, but we all stayed. "Even though none of you left, some of you will not make it," he continued. "Starting from left to right, we want each of you to tell us why you want to be a part of this fraternity," he said. As each person went, one by one explaining why they wanted to be a part of the fraternity, I wondered what I was going to say. I never really thought about joining a fraternity and did not know much about it. In all honesty, I was the one that was approached about it, but I knew I could not say that.

'What can I say? Come on, think, Jay, think!' Each person went, and it quickly got around to me.

"You in the back, why do you want to join this fraternity?" K.C asked. Everyone turned around and looked at me, and I knew I had to say something quick. So, I said the first thing that popped into my head, "God's Plan." Everyone in the room laughed, including K.C and the others. I figured it was the safest thing to say, and no one could argue with God.

"So, you are the comedian, I see," one of the members said. "We are going to have a lot of fun with you," he continued.

Time had passed, and the meeting was coming to an end. I enjoyed the time well-spent and looked forward to what was next.

Finally, K.C said, "We will be in touch with those who made the cut. If you do not hear from us, then, of course, you did not make it, and maybe you should try again next semester," he continued. As we all were walking out, K.C stopped me and said, "John, stick around for a second."

"What's up, K.C?" I asked.

"We just want you to know that you do not have anything to worry because you are in," he said." "Be ready to start in a few days," he added.

I rushed back to share the news with Kiera. Kiera was like my best friend, and I wanted to make sure she was a part of everything that happened with me. As I expected, she was just as excited for me when I told her. A few days had passed, and I was yet to hear from K.C. My anticipation was growing stronger by the minute, thinking about the journey that lied ahead. Kiera had told me to be patient and see what happened next. She was always able to keep my mind off of certain things. It helped a lot that baseball season was coming to an end. We would soon be entering the off-season, so I would have a little more time on my hands. So, I took Kiera's advice and did not pay it any mind.

There was a house party one night, so I figured we would just go there and maybe that would help clear it up even more. The thought of just doing and joining something other than sports had me on tip-toe expectations. Later on that night, I decided to link up with Jesse, Colin, and Derrick. We always rode together when we went to parties. One thing that I appreciated most about this crew was the way we had each other's backs. We looked out for each other through honesty and transparency. I loved my old crew, but with Kevin, Donald, and Brent, there were always some underlying things going on. We were there for each other as well, but in some moments, it felt more like a tight friendship than a brotherhood.

Jesse decided to drive to the party that night since he had the most space. This was fine with me because I knew there was a strong possibility that I would leave with Kiera at the end of the night. A few blocks away from the party, we noticed cars parked on the side of the road and people walking.

"Man, this cannot be from the house party," Jesse said. We pulled beside a group of people walking, and I let the window down to ask about the location of the party.

"Excuse me," I said, getting the attention of the group of ladies. "Are you guys headed to the house party?" I asked.

"Yes," they responded.

"Which house is it?" I asked.

"It is around the corner just a few blocks up, but you may want to park here," she said.

"That is crazy," Derrick said. "I cannot believe this many people would be at a house party," he continued.

"You know what party this reminds me of?" Colin asked.

"What?" we all replied.

"Kita's summer pool party," he replied. Even though I knew exactly why he said it, all I could think about was the great battle that night.

Finally, we were able to park and make our way to the house.

"Shots, shots, shots," echoed from the inside of the house. As soon as we walked in, we were met with shot glasses at the door. Colin was a bit of a drinker, so he quickly grabbed two as the rest of us took one. We walked on in, and there were people all over the place. It was as if the whole college campus was there. Everywhere we walked, there was a different drinking game going on. The back kitchen was a whole dance floor, with the DJ set up by the back door.

"What's up, fellas?" K.C said.

"What's going on, K.C?" I replied. I did not ask him about the fraternity only because I did not want to seem desperate.

"Walk with me John," K.C said.

"So, whose house is this?" I asked.

"This is Prince's house. He's in the frat, too," he replied.

"Let me show you around," he continued. "This room is where you bring a girl that you want to have some one on one time with," he said. "We have this sign that says "Alpha in Progress" we put up when the room is occupied," he continued. As we continued to walk, he stopped again and said, "This room is where it really goes down."

"What do you mean?" I asked.

"This room is for when you want to have some real fun," he replied.

"Real fun like what?" I asked again.

"Let's just say the more, the merrier," he replied. Without asking any more questions about that room, we continued to walk. "This last room I am getting ready to show you is where you guys will be when you start your pledging process tomorrow," he continued.

Excited about the good news, I immediately texted Kiera and told her we were getting started tomorrow. We made our way back to the front, and it seemed that the party got thicker.

Before I knew it, someone screamed, "Power hour!"

"What is power hour?" I asked Colin.

After hearing the question, K.C said, "Power hour is taking the most shots you can take within that hour."

'This is going to be a long night,' I thought to myself.

The next day had come, and I was anticipating how the night would go. I had received a message from K.C that morning telling me to be at Prince's house at 9:06pm and to not be late. I told Kiera I was a little nervous because I had no idea what to expect. When she told me about the stories she heard, it even made me more nervous. She then proceeded to laugh and make light of it. That put me a little at ease.

The evening had arrived, and I received another text from K.C, but this time, there were more people in the group text.

The text read: "Be at J. Prince's house at 9:06pm, bring no more than two cars, and wear white t-shirts." Looking at the group, there were 14 people, not including K.C in the group.

'How are we going to fit 14 people in two vehicles?' I thought to myself. I immediately started a separate group text to have everyone meet at a central location to see who had the biggest vehicle. Someway, somehow, we had to find a way to make it work. We all gathered together and decided to take two trucks since they both had the most space.

We made it to J. Prince's house, and it looked different than the night of the party. Maybe it was because there were not tons of cars in the yard as before.

As we walked into the house, someone yelled, "Line up." We all jumped in line, not knowing what to expect next. As we all stared at each other in line, we noticed J. Prince walking in the room with a big wooden paddle.

'What is he going to do with that?' I thought to myself.

"You all are now property of Alpha Sigma Delta," J. Prince said. "You will now answer by a number and not your name," he continued. "You," he pointed at me, "are number one, which means everything starts with you. If this line fails, it will be because you failed them," J. Prince said. "From this point forward, you all will address us as 'big brother'," he continued. "If you cannot follow instructions, there will be consequences," he added.

"Consequences like what?" one of the guys asked from the line.

"I am glad you asked," K.C said. "Show them the cut position, and I want you to get in it since you asked, Number 10." We all watched as Number 10 got into the cut position and suddenly, *BAM*, the paddle was connecting to the backside of number 10.

"Oh no," Number 10 replied, jumping up and running out of the room.

K.C said in a laughing voice, "And then, there were 13."

I did not know what to think. 'Should I leave behind number 10? It is now or never.'

Before I could gather my thoughts, K.C said, "Let's go ahead and weed out the weak." I knew we were up for a long night.

The night had finally ended, and we all walked out to the trucks. I got dropped off at my dorm room and immediately called Kiera to let her know how it went.

"How did it go?" she asked.

"It was everything you said it would be," I replied as we both laughed.

"How many on your line?" she asked.

With a smile on my face I looked at her and said, "And then there were 8."

chapter

DEAR MAMA

"A mother's love doesn't make her son more dependent and timid;
it actually makes him stronger and more independent."

"**G**ood morning, baby," a sweet, angelic voice awoke me, followed by a soothing kiss.

"Good morning, beautiful," I responded. Things had started to become serious between Kiera and me. It was not often that we spent much time away from each other, but when we did, I missed her deeply.

"How is my Alpha man?" she asked.

"I am wonderful, baby," I replied. Six long weeks of pledging had finally come to an end. March 9th at 2:57am, I crossed those burning sands and became one of the eight newest members of Alpha Sigma Delta.

Kiera was there for me every step of the way. The nights I wanted to quit, she pushed and motivated me to keep going. Even though

47

one of the rules was that we could not be seen with the opposite sex, Kiera always found a way to get to me. If I can be honest, I felt as if this accomplishment was just as much hers as it was mine.

"What are you doing today?" I asked. We both crawled out of the small college bed meant for one, but Kiera and I made it work for the two of us.

"I will probably link up with the girls later since they claim that I never hang out with them anymore," she replied. "What about you?" she asked.

"I have a test to study for," I replied. "If I am going to keep this scholarship, I have to make an 'A' on this test," I added. Pledging took a lot of focus from my books. I found myself studying more of our Greek history than I was for my actual history class. My grades had taken somewhat of a hit, but I knew I would get things back to where they needed to be in the end.

"That is fine," Kiera said as she gathered her belongings to leave. Sealing her departure with a long passionate kiss, I was not even certain that I was ready for her to leave. Nevertheless, as soon as Kiera left, my phone began to ring. It was Jesse and Colin calling.

"What are you doing today, man?" Jesse said. "I have a test I have to study for," I replied.

"Let's hang out for a while before you do that," Jesse said.

"Yeah, man, between Kiera and your fraternity brothers, we barely get a chance to see you," Colin added.

"Just for a little while," I replied. Colin was right. Between spending so much time with Kiera and my fraternity brothers, I barely saw them unless we were passing by.

"Let me take a shower and get dressed, and I will meet you guys at the corner restaurant," I said. I immediately texted Kiera to let her know I would be out with the guys for a little while.

As I made my way up to the corner, I bumped into K.C and J. Prince.

"What's going on, Frat?" K.C said, which was how we all greeted each other.

"Nothing much, just about to get something to eat with the Jesse and Colin," I replied."

"Are you coming to the frat house tonight? We are thinking about throwing a small kickback," J. Prince said.

"Not tonight, man. I have a lot of studying I need to do," I replied. I knew how our kickbacks would eventually end up. They would always start out small but grow into a big block party. It was funny how our kickbacks would start. Somebody would start off by putting $10 on the table, and if you saw the $10, each brother would have to match it. If the table reached a $100, that meant the kickback was in full effect.

"Come on, bro, just come through for a little while," J. Prince said.

"We will make sure you leave at a decent time," K.C added. I knew K.C was lying and would do whatever it took to keep me at the party.

Despite the fact that I knew K.C would keep me there, and I had to study, I looked at them both and said, "I will be there."

The day passed by so fast, and I had yet to crack open my book. By the time I made it back to my dorm from hanging with Jesse, Colin, and Derrick, it was time to head over to the frat house.

'A few hours, Jay,' I told myself over and over until I psychologically got the memo.

I stopped by the frat house, and what was originally supposed to be a small kickback quickly became a big block party, as I feared. Shots after shots after shots! The night seemed like a never-ending process. Waiting on my window to leave, I took the liberty of sneaking out the back while everyone was still partying. It was one o'clock in the morning, and I finally opened my book to study. I knew the only way I would get myself to focus was if I turned my phone ringer off to where I would not hear it. So, I did just that, and in a few hours, I quickly fell asleep with my book still laying on my chest.

The next day had come, and the sunlight shined throughout my room, awaking me from a goodnight's rest. Forgetting to turn my ringer back on my phone, I quickly grabbed it to make sure I did not miss a call from Kiera. To my surprise, I noticed I had 40 missed calls, with a long list of voice and text messages. I decided to listen to the voice messages first since they were from my oldest brother. I pressed play and was immediately shocked and disturbed from what I heard next.

"She is gone, bro, Momma is gone," he said. I immediately called my brother, Gary, to find out what was going on. I could not believe this was happening. I had just talked to her the night before, and she seemed just fine.

'There is no way she is gone,' I said as I tried to convince myself it was all a dream.

"Get here quick, bro, Momma is not doing good at all," he repeated, confirming that it was not a dream, but it was our reality.

I was about an hour and a ½ away from home, but I drove so fast that I made it within 45 minutes. When I arrived at the hospital, I noticed a large amount of my family standing outside. The first person that approached me was my Aunt Ro.

"Get in there, Jay," she said. Without any hesitation, I rushed past my family to find the room that my mom was in. There she was, lying there lifelessly. I had never imagined seeing my mom like this. I watched as my brother and grandmother stood around her crying, and all I could do was stare at the breathing tube shoved down her throat. The machine slowly went up and down, which was the only thing keeping her stable.

"How did this happen?" I asked my brother.

"I had just talked to her the night before, and she sounded just fine," I added.

"She called me in the middle of the night complaining that she was having trouble breathing," Gary said.

"I called 911, and they brought her here," he continued. "Around 6:00am, the doctor said she was no longer breathing on her own, and that she was basically a vegetable."

After listening to my brother, I slowly moved closer to her bedside and grabbed her hand to pray.

"Dear Heavenly Father, I come to you as humbly as I know how. With a sincere heart, God, I know there is nothing that you cannot do. I need you now more than ever. I know my mom is your child, and you are calling her home, but God, I never got the chance to show her how much I love her. I never got the chance to shower her with gifts of love. I never got the chance to take her to her favorite restaurant. Please, God, just grant me the opportunity and give me a little more time. In these blessings, I ask it all. Do this for me, and I will be ever so mindful and grateful to give you all the honor, glory, and praise. In Jesus' name, Amen!"

I sealed my prayer with a kiss to my mom's forehead. Suddenly, her foot began to jump.

"Doctor, doctor," my brother yelled for someone to come into the room. "Her foot just moved," he explained shockingly to the doctor.

"The machine sometimes makes the body react," the doctor replied. Listening to the doctor explain all these medical terms and reactions, I knew it was not the machine that made her move. It was at that point I knew that God not only heard but answered my prayer. The following day, we received a phone call from the doctor explaining to us that the machine was no longer breathing a 100% for my mom. She was now breathing 25% on her own, which meant that God was slowly but surely bringing her back to us. Each day, the percentage increased, and what was said to be impossible was becoming possible with God. By the end of the week, my mom was breathing 100% on her own and was no longer on the machine.

She was now responsive. However, I could notice a change in her reactions. I asked the doctor why her reactions were slower and her behavior was different. Medically, he explained that the lack of oxygen to the brain caused her to lose certain brain cells. In other words, my mom would probably never be the same mentally, but I thanked God that she was still here with us and able to function in her own capacity. When the hospital released her, my siblings and I decided that it would be best that she stayed with my grandmother to help keep an eye on her.

My next thought was how, 'How am I going to do everything I prayed for? How am I going to be able to shower her with gifts of love?' I did not have a job, nor did I come from a wealthy family. I was just a pretty good baseball player, but not even that could help right now. I spent a lot of time commuting back and forth from school to check on my mom. I think it was safe to say that I spent more time at home than I did at school. That alonecaused changes with athletics, classes, and even my relationship with Kiera. I saw less and less of Kiera because I was so focused on being there for my mom. Even my coach later gave me an ultimatum, forcing me to choose between being at practice or home. I loved playing ball. I played it all my life. What made it so fun and exciting was knowing that my biggest supporter was always there. So, I chose to take a break from ball and focus on that time with my mom.

How, just how, was I going to get the money to do all the things I wanted to do for her? Just when I thought that God had done more than enough, I suddenly received a phone call from the business office at my school.

"May I speak to John Rogers?" the receptionist said.

"This is him," I replied.

"This is Mary from the business office, and we have a check here for you," she continued.

"A check?" I replied.

"Yes, it has been up here for a while, and I wanted to let you know," she continued.

"Thanks for letting me know," I replied.

'Where did a check come from for me?' I thought to myself. Surely, it had to be a mistake. However, there was only one way to find out.

I went by the business office as soon as I got back to school.

"I am John Rogers, and I received a phone call saying that I had a check here for me," I said.

"Yes, Mr. Rogers, it has been here for a while. I just need to see your I.D.," she said. I pulled my I.D. out as she slid the check crossed the counter. It clearly had my name on it. I was still in disbelief. I opened it up, and with amazement, I could not believe what I saw. Two thousand, five hundred, and sixty-nine dollars made out to me. I could not believe it. That was when I knew that God would supply all my needs according to his riches and glory.

I quickly took the check to the bank and opened a checking

account. That way, I would not take the chance of losing it or walking with a pocket full of money. I called my mom and told her that I was picking her up for a date.

She laughed and said, "Boy, stop playing."

"I am serious, Mom," I replied. "Just make sure you are dressed and ready to go at 7:00 p.m." I wanted this day to be perfect. I made reservations at my mom's favorite restaurant and made sure I picked up flowers along the way. I stopped by my grandmother's house a little early just to make sure I did not have to help her get ready since she was legally blind. To my delight, when I arrived, there she was in her favorite lavender outfit.

Smiling so graciously, she said, "Okay, son, I am ready for our date." This was something I always wanted to do for her. I walked her to my car and opened the car door like the gentlemen she taught me to be.

Mother's Day, her birthday, and Christmas passed by, and I was able to shower her with all the love I had. Even though so much time had passed by, I knew I was still operating off of borrowed time. I remembered all that I had asked for, and God thought enough of me to answer my prayer. A full year had passed, and my mom found herself back in the hospital for the same reason as before. This particular time, I knew that it was time to give her back to God. As my mom lay there motionless in the hospital bed, I smiled while everyone stared at me in anguish.

"How can you smile when your mom is lying here?" Aunt Ro said. If they only knew what God had done for me, then they would understand why I could smile despite the circumstances.

Emotions were high, and it was hard to explain to them how I could still smile when the world felt like it was tumbling down. To keep the peace, I decided to take a walk and allow them to grieve as they may. A few hours later, I received a phone call from my brother to come back to the room. The doctor wanted to talk to us about taking our mom off of life support. The machine was back to breathing 100% for her, and it had been that way for a few days. He explained that after not receiving the proper oxygen to the brain, even if she did come back to us, she would not be the same. This was one of the toughest decisions I ever had to make in my life.

'Do we keep her on just to see what could happen or do we fully release her to God?' Though I loved my mom so much, I did not want her to suffer any longer. Both of my brothers voted to take her off, but my sister still had hope and was holding on.

There I was, standing there with the deciding vote. All the eyes were on me and what I would decide to do.

"So, what do you say, Jay?" Gary asked. I looked up, and all I could hear was my mom's voice telling me that it was okay to let go.

With tears in my eyes, I looked across the room and told them, "Take her off." We all stayed in the room as the doctor removed all the equipment from her. I leaned over and kissed her on her forehead while her body was still yet warm. Suddenly, she opened her eyes, took a deep breath, and closed them again. That was it! I watched my mom take her last breath. So, instead of being sad and crying with tears of sorrow, I thanked God, from whom all blessings flow, and rejoiced for him allowing me to see it through.

'I love you more than ever, dear Mama.'

7

BREAK UP TO MAKE UP

"Relationships are like glass, sometimes it's better to leave them broken than to cut yourself trying to put them back together."

The hard part was now over, and I found peace by knowing my mom was no longer suffering. My sister was still struggling with the decision we made to take our mom off of life support. I knew it would take some time for her to come to peace with it, and honestly, I was not sure if she ever would.

She called me just about every day, asking me, "Why?" Though there was not anything I could say that would bring her comfort, I trusted that God would reveal it to her in his own time.

The funeral arrangements were now all set, and the only thing left was to inform family and friends. I let all my friends that I was close to know, including Kevin, Donald, and Brent. It had been a while since we all talked, and I figured this would be a better chance than any to settle our differences. I also told Kiera and expected her to be there for me in my time of grief. When she told me that she would not be able to make it, I was shocked. I felt alone and abandoned at the time. Kiera and I's relationship had grown so strong, I just knew she would be there to show her love and support. Nevertheless, I understood she had made plans with her friends.

The day of the funeral had come, and things seemed as normal as could be. My brothers, sister, and I had said our final goodbyes the night before at the wake. Our mom looked so peaceful laying there that I knew we had made the right decision by letting go and letting God take her home. I was able to see family that I had not seen in years. Unfortunately, it seemed like the only time we all got together was when there was a death in the family. Sounds cliché, of course, but it is the truth. As certainly as always, we just made the best out of it.

The funeral did not last long. A few people shared their memories about my mom and songs for preparation for the speaker. I had the opportunity to read a poem that I wrote for her that I titled "Heaven's Flower." My mom loved hearing my poems I would write when I was a kid. After the funeral, we all met in the fellowship hall of the church for the repast. I walked around to mingle with family and friends that I had not seen in a while. Donald never showed, but Brent and Kevin did. It was good to have them there along with Jesse, Derrick, and Colin.

Before I knew it, I looked up, and there she was, looking more beautiful than ever. I could not believe my eyes. She was there at my mom's funeral. She came to support me. Out of all people, it was Lacy.

"Hey, Jay, how have you been?" she asked.

"Despite these circumstances, I have been good," I replied. "I am surprised to see you here," I added.

"I would not dare miss your mother's funeral," she said. "I canceled my whole weekend just to be here for you," she said.

"Well, thank you for coming. I really appreciate you being here," I replied.

"Maybe after all this is over, we can go have a few drinks to catch up," she said.

"I would like that," I said. We then hugged and gazed into each other's eyes like we were back in high school.

"What's up, Lil'Jay?" Brent said as he and Kevin approached me.

"Nothing much, Brent. What's up, Kevin?" I replied. "Thank you guys for coming."

"No problem, bro, you know your mom was like our mom, and we would not miss this for anything," Kevin said.

"Either one of you guys talk to Donald?" I asked.

"I saw him a few days ago, and I told him about the funeral," Kevin said. "What about you, Brent?" I asked.

"No, I have not talked to him, and I am not trying to," Brent said.

"What's been up with you, Lil'Jay, and how is college life?" Kevin asked.

"College is good," I replied. "The baseball team is doing pretty good as well," I continued. "Do you remember Jesse, Colin, and Derrick?" I asked. "They go to school there as well, and we all kick it like we used to do," I added. "I also met somebody that I think might be the one."

"Even better than Lacy?" Brent asked.

"Speaking of Lacy, I saw the way you guys were just looking at each other," Kevin said.

"She just came to speak, man, that is all, and I am sure she has her own thing going now," I said. "I have a great thing going with Kiera now," I added.

"Where is this Kiera?" Brent asked.

"She could not make it," I replied. "She had prior engagements with her friends," I added.

"Wait, you are telling us that she did not come to your mom's funeral because she had plans with her friends?" Kevin said. Kevin had his way of making things sound worse than what they were. Honestly, the more he went on about it, the more he made sense. Maybe it was bad that she did not come and put her friends before me. I really did not know what to think after talking to Kevin.

"Look over there, Lil'Jay," Kevin said, pointing toward Lacy.

"Yes, I see her, but what about her?" I asked.

"That is who you need to worry about right there," he said. I knew what Kevin was trying to do, but I cared about Kiera so much.

'What is a few drinks with an old friend?' I asked myself. 'We are just catching up as old friends, and there is no harm in that,' I tried to convince myself.

"Hey, Lil'Jay," Lacy said as she made her way back over to me.

"What's up, Lacy?" I replied.

"Call me later, after you finish catching up with your guys tonight," she said. In my head, I knew Kiera would not like the fact that I was hanging out with my ex-girlfriend. Before I could give her a fast 'no', what came out was a slow 'yes'.

I decided to leave with Kevin and Brent after the repast. It was good to catch up with them and talk about old times. We went to my mom's house just to relax and have a few drinks.

"So, Lil'Jay," Kevin said.

"What's up?" I replied.

"You plan on seeing Lacy tonight?" he asked.

"Yes, I will invite her over once you guys leave," I replied. "We are just going to chill, nothing more or less," I added.

"Sure, Lil'Jay. You know if she comes here, she is going to want to do more than catch up, right?" he said.

Something in me knew that Kevin was right, but I did not want to think that far ahead or much about it. Lacy and I were done, and I was moving on with Kiera.

'Kiera,' I thought to myself. 'Where is she? Why is she not here by my side? Why is she not here when I need her the most?' These thoughts and questions started to flow through my mind after a few drinks.

Nevertheless, Lacy was on her way, and I was looking forward to knowing how life had been treating her. I must admit that I still thought about her every once and a while. I mean, let's be honest, she was my high school sweetheart.

"Alright, Lil'Jay, we are going to head out and let you get ready for Lacy," Kevin says. "You might want to light candles and put down some rose petals," he continued as we all laughed.

"It was good seeing you, lil'bro," Brent said.

"Love you, lil'bro," Kevin said as we all shook hands.

"I love you guys, too, man. Thanks for coming through," I replied.

As they were leaving, my phone began to ring. It was Kiera finally calling to check on me.

"Hey, baby, how you doing?" she asked.

"I am fine, babe, what are you up to?" I asked.

"I am with my girls now, getting our nails and toes done," she replied. The time in my life when I would need her most, she chose to be with her friends, getting her nails done.

'Should it bother me? Should I even be concerned? Should it even matter?' Thought after thought raced through my head as she continued telling me about her day out with her friends.

"How is the family?" she asked.

"They are okay," I replied.

Looking at the time, I noticed car lights flash through the curtains. I knew it had to be Lacy, so I came up with something to end our conversation early.

"Hey, babe, me, Kevin, and Brent are going to hit a few old spots tonight," I said. "Enjoy your night with your girls," I added. Wow, that was the first time I ever lied to Kiera. It felt so wrong, but I knew if I told her the truth, she would not understand.

"Okay, baby, have fun, and be safe tonight," she said.

I started to feel bad, but that was quickly interrupted by a knock at the door.

"Hey, Lil'Jay," Lacy said as she walked through the door wearing fitted black tights that showed every curve known to mankind. "I hope you do not mind that I stopped at the store and got us something to drink," she continued.

"Not at all," I replied. Even though I was not much of a drinker, I knew a few shots would not hurt to ease my nerves. It was not that I was nervous being with Lacy, but I thought about Kiera and how this would make her feel. Though I felt she was wrong for not being there for me, two wrongs did not make a right. Kiera and I's relationship had stood on honesty and transparency. 'Could this be the turning point of our relationship?'

Nevertheless, a few shots in, and Lacy and I were getting comfortable. It felt like old times between us. I soon forgot all about Kiera and how this may have made her feel.

"You know, I never got the chance to sincerely apologize to you, Jay," Lacy said. "I never meant to hurt you, and I made a stupid mistake," she continued.

"It is okay. We all make mistakes, right?" I replied.

"You are right, and you know what else?" she asked.

"What is that?" I replied.

"I miss you so much, and I cannot get over you," she added.

So much time had passed between us, and it took me a while to get over her. It was always a part of me that I kept hidden away in a secret vault in my heart, which only Lacy had the key to. Nevertheless, the key had now turned, and what came out next was what had been hidden away for a while.

"I miss you, too," I replied. Before I knew it, she leaned in and planted a kiss so softly that it took me back to a place we were once at.

'What am I doing? I cannot do this to Kiera.' I knew in the back of my head that this was wrong, but how could something so wrong feel so right?

"Wait," I said. "There is something that I have to tell you, Lacy."

"What is it?" she asked.

"I have a girlfriend now, and her name is Kiera," I said.

"I understand. How you could not have someone?" she said while leaning back on the couch. "Would you like for me to leave?" she asked. As I sat there and gazed passionately into her eyes, I was surprisingly shocked by even my own response.

"No, I want you to stay the night with me," I said.

"So, what do you want to do tonight?" she asked.

"Let's just make tonight beautiful," I replied as I gently kissed her on the frontal lobe.

chapter

8

LOST DAD

"Every dad, if he takes time out of his busy life to reflect upon his fatherhood, can learn ways to become an even better dad."

A week had passed, and it was time to return back to school and some form of normality. I had spent so much time away from the team and school that I had to go before my coaching staff and also the academic board. I had to explain to them why I spent so much time away and withdrew from so many of my classes. All my life, I had been a great academic student. I graduated number 3 in my class and also had the highest GPA in athletics. Here, I was having to fight to stay in school and not get on academic probation. The only class that I was able to stay in was Fundamentals of Baseball, and that was only because my coach was the instructor.

I also had to face Kiera. I thought about how things would be with us once I made it back to school. How was I going to explain to her what I thought was over suddenly came back? I cared a lot about

Kiera, but there was just something about Lacy that I could not let go of. Lacy and I did have a strong history, and she was my first true love. However, I knew I had to make a decision, and it would come quicker than I would like it to. Lacy wanted to get back together, but was that something I want to jump back into? She was there for me during the passing of my mom. She also apologized for what she did that caused us to break up. Everyone deserves a second chance, right? Then again, Kiera was like my best friend. Even though she did not come to my mom's funeral, she was there for me during the sickness stages. Kiera was also easy to talk to. Sometimes, we would just laugh all night and enjoy each other's company.

I never knew making a decision like this would be so hard. Even choosing a college to continue my baseball career seemed a whole lot easier compared to this. Nevertheless, I would cross that bridge when I got to it.

I decided to stop by my aunt and uncle's house since it had been a while since I saw them. My aunt was my dad's sister. Even though my dad was not around, she would always make sure she stayed in contact with me. When I was a kid, I would always come stay the summer with them and visit during the holidays. I guess she felt bad that her own brother neglected his children, so she always wanted to make us feel welcomed. Then again, maybe she loved us so much that it did not matter what my dad did or not. At this point, it did not matter. All I knew was that my mom was no longer here, and my aunt was the closest person to being a mother figure in my life.

As soon as I arrived at my aunt's house, my cousin Trevor opened the door.

"Mom, Jay is out here," he said as I made my way to the door. I could hear him announcing my arrival as if they anticipated me coming.

"What's up, Jay?" Trevor said.

"Nothing much, Trev," I replied. "What are you guys up to?" I asked.

"Well, Mom is in here cooking, and Dad is watching some old games on the television," he says. "I am trying to figure out if I am going to take this job or not," he continued. I had never seen one person have and lose as many jobs as Trev. Every time I talked to him, he was mentioning how he lost a job and was getting ready for another one. I was not sure if he was just that lucky to find a job so easily or cursed because he lost them just as fast.

Trevor was just a few years older than me, so we spent a lot of time together growing up. Even though we were cousins, he was more like an extended brother.

"Hey, Auntie. How are you?" I asked.

"I am fine, baby. Come give me a hug," she replied.

"Something smells good, Auntie. What are you cooking?" I asked.

"I am cooking your favorite: greens, sweet potatoes, chicken, and cornbread," she said.

"She always tries to cook your favorite when she thinks you will be coming by," Trevor says. "I cannot get her to cook me anything, but if I mention your name, it becomes Sunday dinner," he continued. Sometimes, I could not tell if Trevor was joking or if he was speaking from a jealous place. Regardless, we would just laugh and not pay him any mind.

"Did you know I was coming by, Auntie?" I asked.

"No, but after talking to your dad, I expected you to be by soon," she replied. "By the way, have you talked to him?" she asked.

"No," I replied. "You should call him as soon as possible; there is something important he needs to tell you," she continued. In that moment, I wondered why she wanted me to talk to him so badly.

All this time had passed, and my dad and I had not talked in years. The only memories I had of him were the back and forth, being in and out of our lives.

He would show up for three months out of the year to whoop and beat on my sister and me, then disappear the rest of the year. If I can be honest, the only good memory I had of him was one particular Christmas day. I remember the night my sister and I had only one present each under the tree. We woke up that Christmas morning with a tree full of presents. I really thought that Santa Claus may actually exist but later saw my dad coming from my mom's room.

I had a lot of resentment toward my mom for allowing him to come back and forth in our lives. I never understood the control and power that he had over her. It was as if she was sacrificing her own children.

I remember her stating one day, "I just want you all to have a father." Yet, I quickly realized as I grew older that rules without relationships equals rebellion. I rebelled, and I was trouble, which forced me to make wrong turns early in my life.

Nevertheless, I asked my aunt why I should call him after all these years.

"Just do it for me, baby," she replied. My aunt knew I loved her and would pretty much do whatever she asked of me.

"Okay, I will call later when I get back to my room," I replied. "For now, can I just enjoy this wonderful dinner you prepared just for me?" I said as I looked over at Trevor, adding a little fuel to his jealousy.

After dinner, I decided to head back to my room to relax before calling my dad. Kiera had called and wanted to meet up as well. Now, not only did I had to face my dad, but I also had to face Kiera and was unsure where the road would end.

I decided just to call my dad on the way to my room, so by the time Kiera made it over, we would have time to ourselves. *(Ring, Ring Ring)* I sat there, slightly with anxiety, waiting on my dad to pick up. *(Ring Ring)*

"Hey, son," he answered.

"What's up?" I responded. I could instantly feel myself slipping into a place of anguish and a not so peaceful mood.

"Thank you for calling me, son. How have you been?" he asked.

"I've been well. Auntie said you wanted to talk to me," I replied.

"Yes, son. I first want to apologize for not being there for you the way that I should have," he said. "I always loved you all, but I just could not be there like I wanted to be," he continued. "I always bragged about you and kept every article in the newspaper that was written about you," he says.

At this point, I was not understanding why he was sharing all this with me, but part of me wanted to hear more.

"Oh, yeah?" I responded. "I am glad you were able to read about me because it sure as hell did not make you come see about me," I said. I could feel the anger that I kept hidden away for so many years start to rise.

"I understand that you are angry, son, and I deserve that," he said. "I wish I could make up for lost time, but I cannot," he said.

"So, why now? Why do you want to come back into my life now?" I asked. I was eager to hear his response, only to return with a harsh one of my own. I was not ready for what he would say next.

"Truth is, son, I am dying," he said. As those words left his lips, my heart dropped to my feet, and my chest felt as if I was hit with a giant bolder. I quickly grew silent as I was trying to process what he just said. "Son, did you hear me? I said I am dying," he repeated the traumatizing words again.

"What do you mean you are dying?" I asked.

"I have stage 4 cancer, and the doctor says I only have a few months to live," he added. As much as I wanted to be angry at him, I just could not at the time. How could my heart let me feel for this stranger?

"So, what is next?" I asked.

"I will be home next week since the doctor said there is nothing else they can do," he said. "The treatments are getting too expensive not to work, so I hope to see you when I get home, son," he continued. I did not know what to say or even how to feel in that moment. I wanted to be angry. I wanted to lash out, but I also wanted to show compassion because I knew it was the Godly thing to do.

I pulled up to my room, and Kiera was standing outside waiting on me.

"Okay, I will check on you in a few days," I said. I hung up the phone with my dad to try to get my thoughts and mind together to talk to Kiera.

"Hey, babe, how are you?" Kiera said.

"Hey, I am fine," I said. We greeted each other with a passionate kiss.

"How is everyone doing, and did you get a chance to link up with your old friends?" she asked.

"Everyone is fine, and yes, I did," I replied. "Let's go inside to talk," I said. As we started to make our way to my room, the words of my dad echoed through my mind. I also could not seem to get a grip on what would happen next between Kiera and me.

As soon as we made it to my room, Kiera began to kiss on me as if she was ready to rip me out my clothes.

"Wait, wait, Kiera," I said.

"Can we talk afterward?" she replied while still proceeding to kiss me anxiously.

"I really need to tell you something now," I replied.

"What is so important that it cannot wait until after we finish?" she asked.

"I think we should see other people," I said. Complete silence covered the room as she looked at me puzzled and distraught.

"Why?" she asked.

"I have just been thinking about it a lot, and I think I need time to be alone," I said.

"No, Jay, what is this about?" she asked.

"Kiera, you were not there for me when my mom passed," I responded. Even though that was not the truth, I could not just tell her it was Lacy and that she had come back into the picture.

Without any warning, she then asked, "Is it about Lacy?"

'Wow, did she just read my thoughts? How did she know?'

"Yes, it is Lacy, and the feelings I thought were gone suddenly came out when I saw her," I replied. "One thing led to another, and we slept together," I continued. Tears started to fill her eyes as she stared at me in disbelief. I could hardly believe the words that were coming out of my mouth as well. "I just need time, Kiera," I said. "I just lost my mom, and my dad just told me that he has cancer with only a few months to live," I continued. "It is just so much right now, and it does not seem like you have time for me. Lacy was there for me, and she knows me, so it is only right that I allow her to be there. I just hope you understand, Kiera," I said. She stood up, and I could see the pain in her eyes. Part of me could not believe I was hurting someone that meant so much to me. She walked out of my room without saying goodbye. I did not speak another word.

That night, when I lay down, all I could think about was what my dad was going through. I also thought about what I was going to do next about him. My mom once told me to always pray to have eyes that see the best in people, a heart that forgives the worst, a mind that forgets the bad, and a soul that never loses faith in God. This, by far, was going to be the hardest thing I ever had to do.

A few weeks had passed, and my aunt called to let me know my dad was finally home. She asked me when I was coming to see him, but I just could not find it in me to see him after all this time. For years, I wished for a father, and he was nowhere to be found. I told my aunt that I was not sure if I could see him.Honestly, I did not know what to expect or how I was going to react. All I knew was if I was going to see him, God himself would have to make it clear to me. Miraculously, in that moment, God spoke to me. He reminded me of what he did for me when my mom first got sick. Not only had he granted me more time to spend with her, but he also blessed me with the opportunity to do everything I prayed for. The fact was that God loved me so much as to do that for me; who was I to hold a grudge against my own father?

I later called my aunt to let her know I would go see him. I got in my car and drove over to my grandmother's house, where my dad would stay for the time being. As I walked up to the door, it seemed as if my heart was beating faster and faster with the anxiety of what to expect.

"Hey, baby," my grandmother said as she greeted me with a hug and kiss. "Your dad has been asking about you for a while now," she continued.

I walked to the back room that I remembered sleeping in as a kid. The hallway between the living room and back room never seemed that long as a kid. I felt as if I was walking my own green mile. I opened the door, and there he was, lying there.

"Hey, son," he said while staring at me with a big smile on his face. I stood there trembling, not full of fear but anxiety as I stared back at him. The cancer had eaten away his body so much that I could see every bone structure in his face. His eyes sunk deep into his head. His skin tone was white and pale. His arms, legs, and hands had been decimated away to bones and nails. I could literally count each of his ribs as he laid there wasting away to nothing. I could not believe that this was my dad.

Then, all the pain, hurt, and anger suddenly left my body. My eyes filled up with tears as I greeted him.

"Hey, Dad."

"How are you, son?" he replied.

"I am fine," I responded.

"How is school? And I see that you are still playing ball," he continued.

"School is good, and yes, I am still swinging the bat," I replied.

"I was always proud of you, son, and you have always been my pride and joy," he continued. I sat there and listened to him praise me for my accomplishments and talk to me about things I never knew. I was quickly reminded that no one is perfect, and forgiveness is not just for the other person but also for ourselves.

The truth tastes good when you have had a belly full of lies, and the truth was, he needed me just as much as I needed him. God has a funny way of teaching us lessons. I prayed for a second chance with my mom, and he granted that. Yet in return, I would also have to give my dad a second chance.

I went by my grandmother's house every day to help take care of my dad. We would laugh and talk about many things. I would listen to him tell me funny stories about what I did when I was a little kid. Half the things he shared, I did not remember, but it felt good just hearing him talk about it. I told him about all the things I accomplished through high school, and he would respond with some of the things he did when he played ball as well.

It had gotten to the point that he would not eat unless I was there to feed him.

'Look at me, taking care of my dad. I guess it is true that life does come back full circle.'

"Grab that bag over there for me, son," he said. I walked over to grab the bag that he pointed toward, and it was full of adult diapers.

"You want me to go get Grandmother to come help you change?" I asked.

"No, I want you to do it," he replied.

"Wait, Dad, I love you and everything, but you want me to change your diaper?" I replied.

"Yes, son, I changed yours for many years. Surely, you can change mine once, right?" he said. He then looked at me and said, "What would Jesus do?" We both laughed as I grabbed the gloves to change him.

I decided to head back to the campus to meet up with Jessee and Colin. I was spending so much time with my dad that I had little time for myself. They understood and did not give me a hard time about it. In fact, they took me out just to clear my mind. While we were hanging out, I received a phone call from my aunt.

"Hey, Auntie," I answered.

"Hey, baby, your dad wants you to come see him," she said.

"I saw him earlier today, Auntie, and even changed his diaper," I laughed. "I told him I would be back tomorrow," I continued.

"I know, baby, but he has just been saying he wants to see you," she replied.

"Okay, give me a few minutes," I replied.

"Hey, Jesse, do you mind running me by my grandmother's house?" I asked.

"My dad is asking for me, and it will not take long," I continued.

We pulled up to my grandmother's house, and I told Jessie and Colin that I would be in and out. I walked into the back room and noticed my dad laying back, watching television.

"What's up, Dad? I told you I would be back tomorrow," I said.

"I know, son, I need you to hand me that bag right there," he replied. "Dad, you had me come all the way back over here to change your diaper again?" I asked.

"No, son, just hand it to me," he responded. I grabbed the bag like he asked and watched him search through the pockets. He then pulled out a card and handed it to me.

"What is this?" I asked.

"It is for you son. Just read it," he says. My dad slowly leaned back into his pillow as I opened the card.

> *Congratulations on graduating from high school, son. Sorry I was not able to be there but just know that I am proud of you. I look forward to seeing the man you will become. I still have the newspaper clippings of your games and the ball from your very first home run. I know you did not think I was there, but I stood in the back as I watched you run proudly around the bases. I know you will do great things and be a better man than I am. I cannot make up for lost time, but I want you to know you are the best son any father could ever have. I love you so much, son!*
>
> *Love, Dad*

I slowly closed the card, my eyes blurry from the tears that filled up each eye gland.

"Thanks, Dad. I love you, too," I replied. "But can I ask you a question?" I asked. "Dad... Dad... Dad?!" He was gone!

chapter

9

WHAT THE HEART WANTS

"Do not force someone to remember you all the time. Just stay silent
and let them realize how life will be without you in their life."

My mom was gone, and now my dad was, too. Even though he was not there for me during my adolescent stage, it felt as if we had years of bonding. I was grateful to have shared the short period of time with him. Trying to pick up the pieces of losing both parents within a year's time was difficult, to say the least. Yet life goes on, and it is important not to get stuck in a place of grief. The promises that I made to my mom before she died were still on my mind. Now, for some reason, I wanted to do the same for my dad. It is funny how God can turn things around in a blink of an eye. He allowed me to have closure without any regrets, and for that, I am thankful.

'What now? Where do I go from here?' These were the questions that ran through my head.

The first thing I knew I had to do was get back on the baseball team. As I mentioned before, I spent so much time away from the team, and my coach made me choose. Of course, I chose to be there for my mom and, later, my dad. I knew if I was going to ask for another shot on the team, I would need to be ready to perform. If I was going to get back to the place I once was, I had to work out and train in order to get myself back to tiptop shape. It was not easy because what motivated me the most to play the game I loved was no longer there. My mom was my number one fan and seeing her happy encouraged me to keep going. Nevertheless, I had to find another gear, something that would push me just as much. Kiera and I were no longer talking, but I had Lacy. Lacy, oh, Lacy, I must admit that our relationship was not as strong as it once was. We talked, but it felt like something was missing, and I could not quite put my finger on it. Yet, I had other things to worry about. My number one priority was trying to get myself back to the top of the playing chart.

I decided to wait until after my dad's funeral before I started my workouts. I figured the less distractions I had, the more I could focus on the task ahead. Planning my dad's funeral was a little messier than I thought it would be. I had come to find out my dad owned more things than my siblings and I knew about. My dad was the middle child of six siblings. My aunts and uncles fought over his belongings as if it was not enough that he was dead. They finally asked me if there were anything that I wanted. Truth be told, I was content, and I received the best part of him that anyone could have. I got the chance to share his last minutes of life with him, and that was something that could never be taken away.

The day of the funeral, we all gathered at my grandmother's house for family prayer. The church where the service would be held was right next door. We all planned to walk over together once everyone had arrived. My brothers still held on to the animosity they felt toward our dad for not being there for us. This left me and my sister to attend the service as his children. I understood it, but I wished they would have gotten the opportunity to spend time with him during his last days as I did.

Nevertheless, life went on, and we were here now. The homegoing service turned out to be pretty good. Everyone had great things to say about my dad. I could only think to myself how I wished I could have seen this part of him. The repast was also at the church. I got the chance to meet many family members that I never knew. All afternoon, I received a constant reminder of how much I looked like my dad. I even got the chance to see baby pictures of him, and I must say, we were definitely a spitting image. I walked over to Jesse, Colin, and Derrick, as I made my way through the crowd.

"What's up, Jay?" Colin said.

"Nothing much, man. Ready for this to be over," I replied.

"I know that you are," Derrick added. "First your mom, and now your dad. You are by far the strongest person I know," Jesse said.

"Yo, Jay, look," Derrick said. I turned to see what had suddenly grabbed Derrick's attention. To my surprise, it was Kiera standing there, looking as beautiful as ever.

I walked over to speak since we had not talked in quite some time. To be honest, it felt a little awkward, but I must admit I was glad to see her.

"How are you doing, Kiera?" I asked.

"I am doing fine," she replied. "How about you, Jay?" she asked.

"I cannot complain, and even if I did, it would not change anything," I responded. We talked for at least an hour and it felt good just sharing that moment with her. Lacy let me know she could not make it because she had a prior family event to attend. That was fine because it was not as deep as it was for my mom. Regardless, I appreciated Kiera for coming and supporting me this time. Part of me wished that things ended differently between us. By the vibe of the conversation, I think that she felt the same.

At this point, that was the least of my concerns. My workout started in the morning, and I needed to be 100% focused. I decided to get a personal trainer to help with my strength and conditioning. I had two months before spring training, and I knew the competition would be high. I caught wind that the new recruit was throwing 97-98mph, so I knew I had to come back strong if I was to have any chance. I had not thrown a baseball in months, so my fastball did not have the zest that it once had. I pushed myself extremely hard, day in and day out. I worked out at least three times a day in hopes that I would regain the edge that I once had. Weeks passed by, and it seemed like spring training was quickly approaching. I increased my workouts because I felt like I was not where I needed to be.

The day before spring training, I decided to test my arm strength. I called my recruiting coach to clock me as I threw a few pitches.

"How is it going, Coach?" I asked.

"Going pretty good, Jay," he replied. "We have quite a few good recruits coming in," he continued.

"I heard you guys recruited another pitcher?" I asked.

"Yes, nice kid, and he is throwing just about 98mph," he replied. I knew I had to throw at least 95mph if I was going to have any shot at competing. "Alright, Jay, let's get to it," Coach said.

Here we go. The first pitch I threw was 90mph.

"Still warming up, bud?" Coach asked.

My second pitch was 91mph. I threw another pitch, and it was, again, 91mph.

Did Coach know I was giving it all I had?

"Alright, Jay, last pitch, son, so make it a good one," he said.

"Let's go, Jay," I said while trying to psychologically hype myself up. "Here it goes." And this time, I threw it as hard as I could at 90mph.

"Well, son, I know you have been away from the game for a while, but I can tell there is something missing," Coach said. "If you even want to make the depth chart, I suggest you find that passion," he continued. "Good luck to you, son," he says as he patted me on the back and walked away. Coach's words ringed through my head as I walked back to my dorm room. I had lost my passion when my mom passed away. How could I find something that physically died inside of me? Everything I was or would be was motivated by my mom. I hated to say it, but my desire to be a professional baseball player was no longer there. I was done.

I tossed and turned, thinking about how my life would look without playing ball. I never thought this day would come, at least not this quickly. Yet here I was, and all I could think about was what was next.

I broke the news to Jesse, Colin, and Derrick. Colin and Derrick had previously decided to not play football anymore as well, but Jessie stayed on the basketball team. Jesse tried his best to change my mind, but I could not shake the fact that my love for it no longer existed. I would only play because I had the athletic ability to do so. Now, even that was questionable.

I called Lacy in the hopes that she would give me a sense of comfort, but she did not answer. I knew I could call Kiera, but was it the right thing to do? Would she even want to talk to me? I contemplated back and forth on what to do, and suddenly my phone rang. To my surprise, it was Kiera. It was as if she could feel that I needed her in that moment. Without hesitation, she rushed right over to sit with me.

"Hey, Kiera," I said as we greeted each other with a hug. We talked all night, just like old times. She made me forget all about baseball and look at the big picture, which was my happiness.

"You know what, Jay?" Kiera said.

"What is that?" I replied.

"I miss this part of us," she said. Truth be told, I missed it, too. In fact, I missed everything about her. Her smile, laugh, hugs, and kisses.

"Well, it is getting late, and I know you have tons of things to do tomorrow," Kiera said. Deep down, I was not ready for her to leave, but I knew it was best since Lacy was coming this weekend.

"Okay, thanks for coming by Kiera, I really appreciate you," I responded. We hugged, and she kissed me ever so softly on my cheek.

The next day had come, and Lacy was on her way. We had plans to attend a fraternity party that we were having that night. When she arrived, we quickly made up for lost time. I really did not care for the distance between us, but it was our reality. I showed her around our campus since she had never seen it. I asked her if she would consider coming to school here, but she was very clear that school was not her cup of tea. I talked to her about my future without baseball, but she did not seem very interested, to say the least. We decided to go to the party early to avoid parking and walking blocks away, yet we still ended up walking quite a distance from the house.

We made it to the house, and I introduced her to many of my fraternity brothers.

"What's up, K.C?" I said.

"Nothing much, Jay," he replied. "Let me talk to you for a second,

Jay," he said. K.C pulled me to the side as if he was worried about something. "Yo, bro, you know Kiera is here, right?" he asked.

"I did not know, but I figured she would be," I replied.

"You know that girl is still in love with you," he continued. As I stood there listening to K.C talk to me about Kiera, I knew that I still loved her, too, yet here I was with Lacy.

I walked back to the front to make sure Lacy was okay. I then saw Kiera staring at me as if she wanted to bite my head off and love on me at the same time.

"Hey, Kiera," I said.

"Hey, Jay," she replied.

"So, this is Kiera," Lacy said.

"Yes, this is Kiera," I replied.

"Come on, Jay, I am ready to go," Lacy said.

"Why do you want to leave so early when we just got here?" I asked. Without replying, Lacy walked outside, leaving me standing there confused. I walked outside to find Lacy standing in the street with her arms folded.

"What is wrong, Lacy?" I asked.

"That was so disrespectful, Jay," she replied.

Confused as to why she had an attitude, I asked her, "What did I do?"

"You are standing there making googly eyes with your ex-girlfriend while I am standing there," she says. "If you want to be with her, then just say that," she continued. I was not sure about the googly eyes that Lacy was referring to, but it was quite certain that with Kiera was where I wanted to be.

We made it back to my room after riding back to the campus in complete silence. In the midst of the silence, I began to think about a lot. I reflected back on the words of my coach about finding my passion again. Truth was, Kiera was my passion. Everything in me loved Kiera.

"Lacy," I said.

"I know, Jay, you do not have to tell me," she said. "I know that you are still in love with her," she continued.

"I am," I responded. "I am sorry, Lacy," I said.

"No need to be sorry. The heart wants who the heart wants," she replied.

"I will leave first thing in the morning," she continued. I did not want to hurt Lacy. In fact, I felt bad because she did mean a lot to me. I knew I could not give myself to her fully while knowing that my heart belonged to Kiera.

"Goodbye, Lacy," I said as I walked off, leaving her to herself.

chapter

10

FOR BETTER OR FOR WORSE

"Our greatest pains and disappointments never come from our adversaries.
They come from those we choose to love, those we give anything for and
those who were blind to the risk and consequences of ever hurting us."

An easy and featherlike life sounds so amazing, doesn't it? Yet instead, we carry so much weight around with us. When I think about how that weight may look physically, I am quickly reminded of when I was younger, carrying a backpack full of stolen goods. Now, the weight of life feels like a backpack full of stones. Each stone symbolizes rejection, heartbreak, family division, and many other struggles. Every morning, it feels as if the weight grows heavier and heavier. The next phase of life almost feels impossible because the last one was so demoralizing. I cannot imagine how to look or even move forward with the heaviness I feel. What is disheartening is that many of us carry this invisible backpack without even recognizing it.

Kiera and I had now been married for four years. What I envisioned would last forever started to slowly drift away like leaves in the fall weather. Collectively, we had been together for 13 years. Thirteen years of ups and downs, ins and outs, roller coaster after roller coaster. It seemed as if the break-ups and make-ups were inevitable. One thing that always remained was the love we had for each other. We even tried separating and seeing other people but were quickly drawn back together like two magnets. Most importantly in these 13 years, two beautiful girls were born. There was one between Kiera and I, and the other one was a surprise from Lacy. Apparently, Lacy got pregnant before we officially called it quits. This was the first issue that came about between Kiera and me.

Lacy tormented me and Kiera so badly after our daughter was born. For eight years, I was dragged in and out of court just to have visitations with my daughter. I saw a side of Lacy that I never knew existed.

I guess it is true what they say: "A bitter woman can be a man's worse nightmare."

In this case, it was a horror film that never seemed to end. I could tell that Kiera was becoming overwhelmed with all the wicked antics from Lacy. She was putting a lot of strain on my and Kiera's relationship, and there was nothing I could do about it. I spent my first night behind bars because of Lacy. A place that I promised my mom that I would never end up. It was at that moment I knew I had to do something different. The lies and manipulation were reaching their peak, and no matter what I told the judge, he continued to give her a slap on the wrist.

Kiera and I decided to pursue full custody of my oldest daughter, which we eventually won. I must say, it was one of the hardest things I ever had to do. What made it so difficult was that I had to represent myself during the court matter. That alone was another issue within itself. Ten long hours of a custody battle in court was draining. I must admit hearing the judge say my daughter was going home with me was worth every second. I knew it would take some time to adjust to the change.

At first, I just wanted to be the father I never had growing up. Now, I can honestly say I want to be a great dad because that is what I desire to be. Nevertheless, I finally had my family all together. I had a beautiful wife and my two most precious gifts. What more could a man ask for? A question that would soon be quick with an answer.

There was so much tension in our home between Kiera and my oldest daughter, Jersey. I did not understand where all the tension came from when they were once so close. I remember times on the weekends that I would get Jersey, and she would want to spend more time with Kiera than me. I would often have to sleep on the couch because Jersey would cry to sleep with Kiera. It was puzzling to once see them share so much love, to now question if they even liked each other.

I decided to talk to Kiera to see what I could do to make the situation better between Kiera and Jersey.

"Hey, babe, how was your day?" I asked.

"It was fine," Kiera replied.

"Great, do you mind if we talk?" I asked.

"Sure, what about?" she responded.

"I want you and Jersey to work on building a better relationship," I said. "When was the last time you talked, hugged, or even told her that you loved her?" I asked,. As we sat there, I could tell by Kiera's face that she was getting annoyed. I did not want to press the issue too much, so I eased up to allow her to respond. I was then shocked by her response.

"I do not want to build a relationship with her," Kiera said. "I do not want to be her mom," she continued. I could not believe my ears. Did she mean what she said, or was she speaking out of anger and frustration? Regardless, how could my very own wife have so much animosity towards a child. Not just any child but my flesh and blood. Someone that she once built a complete bond with. Truth is, it was her idea to pursue custody of Jersey. I could not make any sense of it. Where did things go wrong?

I walked out of the room, leaving Kiera to herself. I tossed and turned all night as her words echoed loudly in my head. I knew this situation could not be of God because He is not the author of confusion. I prayed for guidance because I knew only God could help us in this family affair. The next morning I got up and went through my normal routine. I made sure my girls were dressed and ready for school. I prayed over them every morning before they left the house and kissed my wife goodbye.

I went to work with a lot on my mind. I knew I had to figure out how to get over the mountain with my family. I desired my family so much that I would do anything to keep us together. I suggested family counseling, but Kiera was against it for some reason. Honestly, I felt like we needed professional help, but Kiera and I needed to be of one accord. How could I get us there? What could I do to ensure that this family stayed together? I decided to sit and have a family meeting once I got home from work. I figured the best way to get an understanding with each other was to address how each of us felt.

I started off by giving my take on the tension in the house. I also shared my vision of how important it was for us to love and support each other.

"Everyone here has a role to play," I said. "Everyone's role is important, even you, baby girl," I addressed my attention toward my youngest daughter. "What would you like to say?" I asked my youngest daughter, Mya.

"I want us to love and be happy, Dad," Mya said. Hearing my baby girl speak always touched my heart. She had the most pure and angelic spirit.

"That is why we are here, baby girl," I replied. "We are so happy you are a part of this family," I added.

"What about you, Jersey? What would you like to share?" I asked. Being slow to speak, I knew she had a lot on her mind. "You do not have to be ashamed or scared to talk to us," I said. "We are your family, and I assure you that this a safe place," I added.

"I want Kiera to spend time with me like she does with Mya," she said. "I want her to play games with me and show me that she cares," she continued. I could see the pain in her eyes as tears began to build up. After the custody hearing, Jersey saw less and less of her biological mother, Lacy. Lacy had moved away and kept little contact with Jersey. I knew that she missed her mom, and it did not help to see her younger sister get all the love from someone who vowed to be a mother figure in her life.

"Is there anything else you want to see or share with us?" I asked.

She then looked up at Kiera with tears in her eyes and said, "I just want you to love me."

Immediately, my heart dropped to the bottom of my soul. I could not hold back the tears as I watched my daughter pour out her soul. There was raw realness and authenticity of pure emotion. I took a moment to gather myself and regain control of the moment. I then looked over at Kiera and asked her if she would like to address what Jersey said. In that moment, it was time for Kiera to show us her heart. The atmosphere was set, and this was going to be the turning point in our family.

Kiera then coldheartedly looked at Jersey and said, "I can't." I was stunned and completely caught off-guard by her response. I did not know what to say, but this family meeting was adjourned.

The next day, I knew something would have to give. We could not continue to go on like this. I decided to sit down and have a one-on-one conversation with Kiera.

"Hey, baby, we need to talk."

"I think we do as well," she replied.

"You can go first," I said. I felt good about the fact that she wanted to talk but was not sure what would come out.

"I want a divorce," she said. I never thought I would hear those words in my life. My heart shattered immediately. I suddenly could not breathe, and my chest had tightened up so badly it was as if I was having a heart attack. I knew things were not perfect, but it was not not bad enough to throw in the towel so soon. It was as if she already had one foot in and one foot out.

"Why?" I asked.

"I am not happy, and this is too much for me," she said. I was puzzled, shocked, and in disbelief at what was coming out of Kiera's mouth. Yes, we had our share of issues, but what marriage didn't?? I begged Kiera to reconsider, but it seemed like she was so determined to be apart.

"I have a suggestion," I said. "Let's give ourselves space and time to gather our thoughts and later come back to discuss what we will do moving forward."

Each day that passed by, all I could do was think, 'How? How did things get so bad between us? How did I not see this coming? Was I preparing for forever while she was planning her exit the whole time?' I tried to stay positive, but the cloud of divorce hung over my head. I even questioned myself as a man and a father. Did I make the right decision by bringing my daughter here? Should I send her back to Lacy? I just did not know what to do at this point, and it felt like my whole life was crumbling down. I found myself slipping in and out of depression, and I literally could not eat or sleep. The thought of not having my family destroyed every part of my soul. I loved Kiera so much, and I would often reference her as my heart in human form. Was I reaping what I sowed all those years ago? For all the broken hearts that I was responsible for, could this be my punishment? Question after question rambled through my mind. I honestly felt like I was next door to going insane. Deep down inside, I knew I had to keep it together because I had two beautiful daughters that depended on me.

A week passed by, and it felt like 10 years. I had not heard from Kiera. I wanted to call and talk to her, but we both agreed to give each other time and space. I felt like a failure. I failed myself, I failed my family, and most of all, I failed God. He gave me the responsibility of a family, and I mismanaged what he blessed me with. I wondered if Kiera thought about me as much as I thought about her. We were no longer in college, and things were supposed to be different between us. The vision of me and Kiera standing hand and hand at the altar replayed over in my head. For better or for worse, richer or poorer, sickness and in health, until death do we part? I meant every word I said to her, yet it was quite clear to me that she did not.

A few weeks had passed by, and the anxiety started to creep in. Kiera and I had set a date that we would come back to the table and talk about what we would do moving forward. For the first time in my life, I felt unsure of what the future may hold. When I played baseball, I knew what to expect. The moment I decided not to play anymore, I knew I would not go back. This situation was different because my whole world revolved around my family. Everything I was and everything I would be was because of them. Whoever thought I would love so hard? That I would love someone more than life itself? God has a funny way of teaching us lessons. Could this be my lesson to learn? Surely, God would not punish me so harshly, would he? Regardless, I was there, and I had to face this head on.

The day had finally come that me and Kiera set aside to talk. The anticipation of what was next overtook my emotions. What would be our fate? I was not able to focus at work because my mind was scattered in so many different places. On a normal day, time seemed to be going slow, but today, it flew by so fast. Before I knew it, 5:00pm had come, and it was time for Kiera and me to meet. I sat at the house waiting anxiously for Kiera to show. I said a few prayers and asked God for peace in whatever direction he chose to take us.

Suddenly, I heard a car door shut.

'There she is,' I said to myself. 'Okay, Jay, relax and breathe,' I attempted to gain control of my anxiety.

"Hey, baby," I said as she walked through the door.

"Hey," she said, greeting me with a hug and kiss.

'That is a good sign,' I thought to myself.

"I miss you so much," I said. "I miss you, too," she replied.

"I have been miserable without you," I said. "I do not know what the future may hold, but I do know I do not have one if you are not in it," I continued. "What I am trying to ask you, baby, is are you coming home?" By this time, tears were beginning to flow between Kiera and me both. It was quite obvious that we both loved each other. The ball was now in her court, and she knew where I stood. Would we sink in this life of quicksand, or would we dig deep and rally? Only time would tell as we walked through this Valley.

J. Kenkade
PUBLISHING

Ghostwriting

We write your story for you!
You're still the Author.

www.jkenkadepublishing.com/ghostwriting
(501) 943-8300

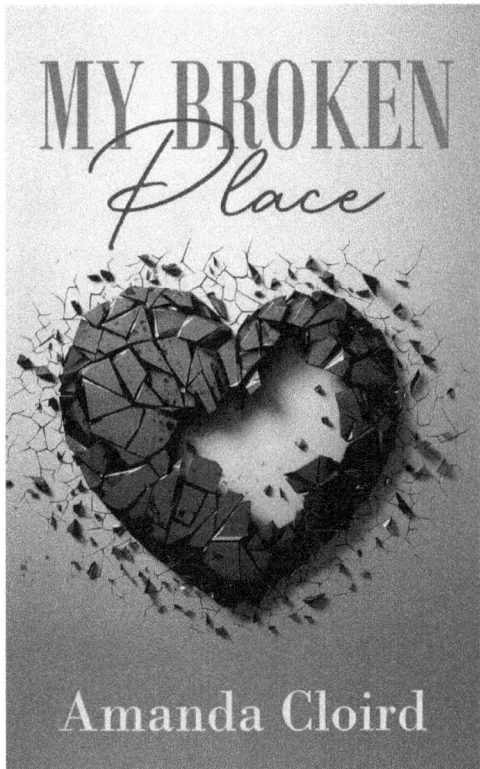

MY BROKEN *Place*

Amanda Cloird

Also Available from
J. Kenkade Publishing

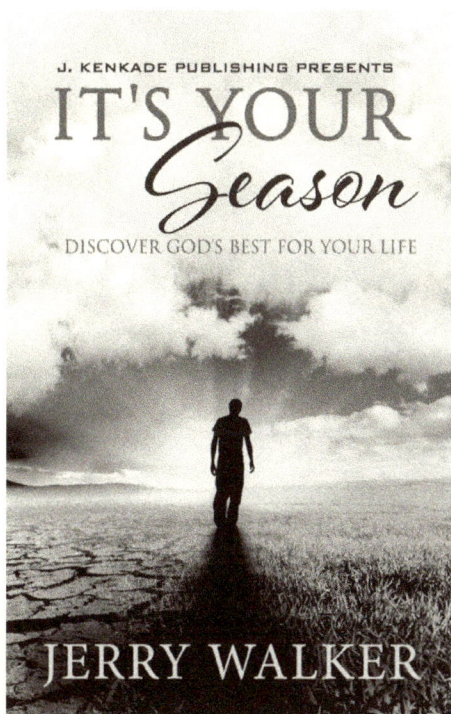

J. KENKADE PUBLISHING PRESENTS

IT'S YOUR

Season

DISCOVER GOD'S BEST FOR YOUR LIFE

JERRY WALKER

Also Available from
J. Kenkade Publishing

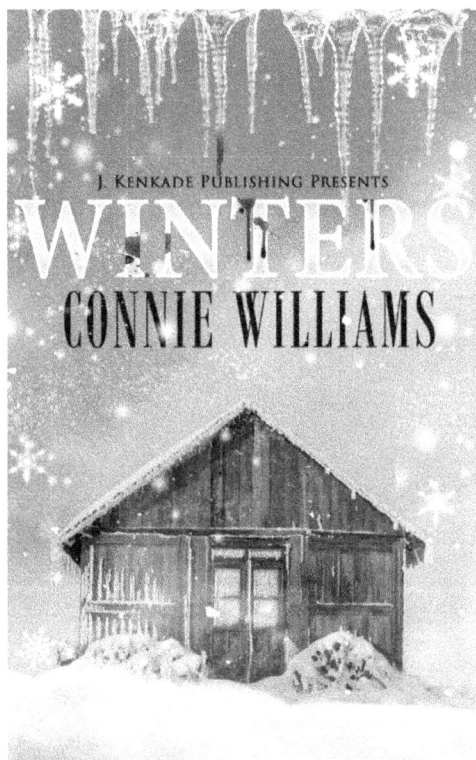

J. KENKADE PUBLISHING PRESENTS
WINTERS
CONNIE WILLIAMS

www.ingramcontent.com/pod-product-compliance
Lightning Source LLC
Chambersburg PA
CBHW030958090426
42737CB00007B/594